"I chose sober because I wanted a better life. I stay sober because I got one."
~ Anonymous

"You have to break down before you can breakthrough." ~ Anonymous

"If you do what you've always done, you'll get what you've always gotten."
~Tony Robbins

"When I got sober, I thought giving up was saying goodbye to all the fun and all the sparkle, and it turned out to be just the opposite. That's when the sparkle started for me."
~ Mary Karr

HOW TO QUIT ALCOHOL LIKE A BOSS AND LIVE A LIFE OF S O B R I E T Y

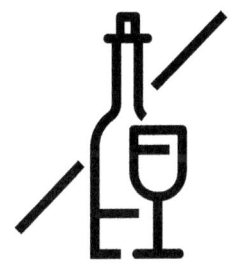

JESSICA M CLARK

My diary entry from the day I decided enough was enough.

5 minute journaling

The end of last week was pretty tough for some reason. I always feel the need to damage my life when things are going well. And guess who is always to blame... ALCOHOL! Well by blame, it's obviously me choosing to drink. I just know I would be a much nicer, more successful person if I stopped. I feel so ashamed for not only me, but for Ollie, he really deserves the world, not some sad excuse for a girl who can't control her drinking! My nan is still in hospital but seems to be on the mend. I pray she gets better soon. Getting old sucks!

Night y.

Daily Journal

DAY Sunday
DATE 29.10.23

GOALS
1. finish a few journals
2.
3.

SELF CARE
Water: ●●●●○○○○
Exercise: N/A
Yoga/stretch: None
How I'm feeling: down

THINGS TO DO
- Washing
- Journals
- tidy

TIME | TASK/EVENT
12:00 | drive home

DON'T FORGET
- Georgia from 01/01.

NOTES

QUOTE OF THE DAY
IF PEOPLE ARE DOUBTING HOW FAR YOU CAN GO, GO SO FAR THAT YOU CAN'T HEAR THEM ANYMORE.

And for those of you unable to read my handwriting in the photo...since I barely can.

Sunday, 29th October 2023

The end of last week was pretty tough. For some reason I always feel the need to damage my life when things are going well. And guess who is always to blame...alcohol! Well by blame, It's obviously me choosing to drink. I just know I would be a much nicer, more successful person if I stopped. I feel so ashamed for not only me, but for Olie, he really deserves the world, not some sad excuse for a girl who can't control her drinking!

My nan is still in hospital but seems to be on the mend. I pray she gets better soon. Getting old sucks!

Night
X

Contents

	Introduction
Phase 0	Enough is enough
Phase 1	Back to basics
Phase 2	Embrace the loneliness
Phase 3	Rediscovery – date yourself
Phase 4	The healthy stuff
Phase 5	Financial awakening
Phase 6	The hard truths
Phase 7	Reaping the rewards
Phase 8	Never look back

Introduction

Are you a serial offender, or maybe your relationship with alcohol isn't in complete shambles, but you'd like to quit anyway, as you've realised it's not benefiting your life? Well, you've come to the right place, or should I say the right book. This book is for those who want to break free from the toxic cycle of alcohol and live a healthier, more fulfilling life. I quit drinking just over one year ago because after fifteen years of getting black-out drunk, waking up filled with regret, anxiety and feeling awful about the choices I was making, I decided it was no longer serving me and there had to be a better way forward than the toxic cycle I was in. Your situation may be somewhat different to mine, as I know everyone's relationship with alcohol is personal, however for some reason or another, you've felt it's necessary to read this book and I'm glad you're here.

Introduction

Whatever your relationship is with alcohol, it's unlikely to be a good one if it's brought you here, and you're ready for a change.

I should start by saying that I'm not a qualified life, sober or addiction coach and if you feel you would benefit from professional help because you're severely addicted to alcohol, I hope my book can help you, however, I feel this might not be the right place for you and seeking professional help might be a better choice in your situation.

> "Whatever your relationship is with alcohol, it's unlikely to be a good one if it's brought you here and you're ready for a change."

I've written this book in the hope of helping the "middle-lane" drinkers. The individuals who don't necessarily depend on it every day but have "alcohol use disorder" or are nearing this stage. The individuals who feel they cannot be in certain situations without drinking alcohol, don't know when to call it a night and have zero control. The individuals who frequently drink more than they plan to, feel guilty after drinking, experience blackouts, lie about their drinking or downplay the severity of it, often drink alone when they're not feeling great and will choose to drink over participating in other activities or hobbies. If you've nodded your head a few times whilst reading the above, then good. You're in the right place.

Introduction

You may be an individual who doesn't fall into these categories either, and perhaps you're simply just optimising a life without alcohol in it. One thing I do know is that if you've ever thought about removing alcohol from your life, the likelihood is it's because you have a problem with it (big or small) and it's not adding any value to your life.

> "Reflecting on the past year, I've never felt more present, happier or healthier."

According to the World Health Organization (WHO), alcohol consumption contributes to 2.6 million deaths each year globally, as well as to the disabilities and poor health of millions of people. As someone who has realised how harmful alcohol use can be, my intention for this book is to share valuable tips, and often some hard truths with individuals who want to make a positive change in their lives and feel drinking alcohol is preventing them from doing so. Thank you for being here. I hope my book helps you and provides comfort during your sobriety journey. So many people have a poor relationship with alcohol, so believe me when I say that you are far from alone.

Reflecting on the past year, I've never felt more present, happier or healthier. For anyone who is sober curious, I hope this book gives you the final nudge you need to go for it. Even if it's just for one, two or three months, I promise you, you won't regret it.

Introduction

Throughout this book, I try to cover all the things I've learned during my first year of sobriety, the hard truths about being sober around loved ones and some lifestyle changes you'll potentially need to make to give this a real shot. Choosing to live a life of sobriety can be challenging at first. Still, once you've learned how to navigate various situations, it is the most liberating feeling because putting yourself and your needs above anything else is the ultimate superpower. Becoming the best version of you means you're in the best place to show up and support your loved ones, succeed in your career, reach your health and fitness goals, discover new passions and lead an overall healthier lifestyle, which alcohol can sometimes (if not always) get in the way of achieving.

> "Putting yourself and your needs above anything else really is the ultimate superpower."

I hope you enjoy reading, but most importantly, after you finish this book, you feel empowered to give sobriety a real shot like the boss I know you are. I hope the points I run through leave you feeling prepared for the challenges you might face. I am so excited for you to embark on this next chapter of self-love. Buckle up, because it'll be your best chapter yet, and I hope you'll never look back.

Phase 0
Enough is enough

It's taken me a long time to accept that my relationship with alcohol isn't a healthy one and to truly understand that it's ok and that alcohol isn't for everyone. I decided to write this book one year into my sobriety journey in the hope of helping others navigate their way to a healthier lifestyle which doesn't involve booze and realise that just because you have an unhealthy relationship with alcohol, it doesn't make you a bore, failure, an alien, loser and the rest. It makes you an average person who wants to live a healthier, more present life which involves more self-love than you could have ever imagined possible for yourself. To be able to help you, I feel it's necessary for you first to understand a little about me, my journey and my ongoing struggles with alcohol, which may or may not resonate with your own experiences.

Phase 0 - Enough is enough

Without sounding cliché, I feel if I can break up with alcohol and accept it's not for me, you most certainly can, too. I hope this book reminds you that you're not alone and that so many people feel the way you might be feeling right now, including myself, just over twelve months ago. The person I am today doesn't recognise the person I was twelve months ago. The Jess from twelve months ago was messy, reckless and often uncontrollable. She needed someone to pick her up and take care of her, and when she realised that person was herself, the game changed. On that note, here's to my somewhat messy past...

> "She needed someone to pick her up and take care of her, and when she realised that person was herself, the game changed."

I grew up in suburban Bristol with my mum, dad and two older sisters. Being the youngest of three, I always felt I was missing out if I couldn't participate in all of the things my older sisters were able to, which meant I often got my way and was trusted to do things much younger than I probably would've been trusted to do so if I was the first child. When it got to me, it was as though my parents thought, "Eh, the other two turned out fine, so what could go wrong?". My 14–15-year-old self thought this was amazing and took full advantage. I would go to parties, drink alcohol, smoke cigarettes, go clubbing and experience the hardcore, fun, party lifestyle much earlier than most teenagers

Phase 0 - Enough is enough

get to. Yes, this was great at the time, but as I'm now approaching thirty and reflecting, I wish I had taken the time to enjoy my teenage years carefree and present without needing to "depend" on alcohol to have fun or prove myself to people who had zero benefit to my life. With that being said, we learn through our experiences, and for some reason or another, I had to get that out of my system and make the mistakes I did to truly appreciate who I am now. Half the time, my parents didn't know what I was up to and trusted me to make wise choices, so I can't knock them for that – I was young, carefree and often thought it was a game to see how far I could take it and what I could get away with. As a teenager, we often feel we're invincible. Only as we get older do we realise maturity often comes with learning from past mistakes, outgrowing our vulnerabilities and overcoming specific challenges.

"I'm never drinking again…"

As I approached my late teens, I really struggled with my mental health and couldn't figure out who I was or what I wanted out of life. Don't get me wrong, I'm not saying I have everything figured out now, far from it actually, but I definitely have a sense of purpose, direction and trust in myself to make the right decision for me, which I definitely didn't have before. The frustration of not having anything figured out and a real lack of purpose in my life often led to spending

Phase 0 - Enough is enough

almost every weekend getting sh*t faced (excuse my French) with friends as it was a good distraction and meant the "real, serious, boring life stuff" could be put to the back of the priority list.

The endless nights out meant living in constant fear and regret the whole of Sunday. This often involved profusely crying to my boyfriend at the time, wishing I wasn't such a mess, and quoting the famous (wait for it) "I'm never drinking again". This was only until the following weekend when the vicious cycle would repeat itself. Yes, I certainly had a lot of great times and lifelong memories made with friends and not all weekends were bad, but I certainly had a lot of "I wish I hadn't done that" moments and sadly, they're the ones which indent in our brains, as it seems much easier to beat ourselves up over our bad choices than to give ourselves grace, especially at such a young age. I want to say this cycle ended as I approached my early to mid-twenties, but sadly, it just got worse.

"It seems much easier to beat ourselves up over our bad choices than to give ourselves grace."

I decided to move to London and felt like a kid in a playground. I had a huge, new, magical city to explore where it didn't matter what day it was, if you wanted to party, there was always a place to go and people very happy to join you. My job at the time meant the hours I

Phase 0 - Enough is enough

worked varied. Some days I would work until late in the evening, which often resulted in me and a couple of colleagues going for a drink after our shift ended. It didn't matter what day of the week it was; if we worked the late shift together, we'd always "Go for one", which, of course, was never just one. Before I knew it, I would wake up in a frenzy, feeling awful after getting home at 4-5 a.m., anxious about what I'd gotten up to the night before since, as you guessed it, I often couldn't remember. I would then have to race to work as often this behaviour resulted in me turning up late, looking and feeling horrendous.

> "Before I knew it, I would wake up in a frenzy, feeling awful after getting home at 4-5 am, anxious about what I'd gotten up to the night before."

Some people manage to hide their hangovers, but sadly, I was never one of them - it would be written all over my face and usually involved running to the bathroom to be sick every 10 minutes. My hangovers felt as if I was experiencing the damage the alcohol was doing to my body in real-time. My body wanted to reject it as fast as it could. I've never felt unhealthier than on the days when I would be led in bed, not being able to eat or drink a thing without vomiting, head pounding, uncontrollably sweating, and my mental health rapidly declining as the day went on and I slowly started to regain memory of the night before. Not to mention the sickening, sour smell of one-day-old booze and musky tobacco…puke.

Moving to a new city is very exciting, and it's a chance to reinvent ourselves. However, as I continued this self-destructive cycle, it started to dawn on me that the endless drinking and partying were damaging almost every aspect of my life in one way or another. I wasn't heading in the right direction or making myself proud.

> "The drinking and partying were damaging almost every aspect of my life, in one way or another."

One weekend in particular stands out more than most. I had planned to go home to Bristol to celebrate my Dad's birthday, and the whole family, including my Grandparents, Auntie, Uncle and Cousins, were going for Sunday lunch to celebrate. I chose not to spend the weekend in Bristol as I often would, as I had planned to go out with some work friends on Saturday night in London, so I agreed to travel back early Sunday morning instead to make the meal. After telling myself I would only have a few drinks, the Saturday night ended as usual. I woke up in a panic at midday the next day, hysterical because I had slept through my alarm, missed my coach and wasn't going to make my Dad's birthday meal. I had spent way too much money and couldn't remember how I got home or at what time. I felt as though I'd been run over by a bus…repeatedly. And to be

Phase 0 - Enough is enough

honest, part of me wished I had been. I frantically booked the next coach whilst my family delayed the meal, and everybody waited for me to arrive before ordering. I arrived and could hardly eat my meal or hold a conversation, so I might as well not have been there. My body was present, but I certainly wasn't. I don't think anybody noticed and thought it was a minor mishap, which is positive; however, I cried the whole journey back to London later that day because, yet again, I had made a poor choice, which was self-inflicted and made me feel like a failure.

> "Yet again, I had made a poor choice which was self-inflicted and made me feel like a failure."

Yes, mistakes happen, and this could have happened to anyone. Still, the more these types of scenarios occurred, the more I would ask myself why I wanted to continue living this way and would beat myself up for acting so recklessly, over and over again. Some nights were inevitably much worse than others. Sometimes, I'd lose my bag, so I'd wake up with no phone, money or belongings, or I'd get home to find I had smashed my entire phone screen, which I'd later brush off once I'd gotten it repaired. But every time I'd let myself down due to the amount of alcohol I was drinking, the more I slowly started to despise myself. Sometimes I'd let other people down, but the person I'd let down every single time was myself. Almost missing my Dad's

Phase 0 - Enough is enough

birthday meal probably seemed like a very harmless mistake from an outside perspective, but in my head, this was the same scenario I'd dealt with many times. Another problem was caused, which could have easily been avoided if I just learned how to moderate my drinking and when to call it a night. Spending so many days in bed, unable to eat or drink without being sick, and not wanting to speak to anybody as I felt so depressed. Anxious about the previous night's events, and terrified to check my bank balance as there was a 99% chance I had gone into my overdraft from buying stranger's shots, just so they would join my high, again, as usual.

"The same scenario I'd dealt with many times over."

A lot of my drunken nights I struggle to remember, but I'll share another which truly made me feel the lowest of the low. One of my best friends and I would have a joint birthday party most years since our birthdays were only two weeks apart. Roughly five years ago, we had our standard joint party, which we'd usually host at her parent's house since there was a big, lovely garden, perfect for summer events and big enough to fit all our friends comfortably. There are 14 of us in the main group who have been friends for as long as I can remember, and I'm incredibly grateful to have them in my life. The day after our birthday party that year, I

Phase 0 - Enough is enough

honestly thought I was going to lose some of them, and I wouldn't have blamed them - messy drunk Jess strikes again.

As our birthdays are in the middle of summer, the parties usually start in the early afternoon to take advantage of a whole afternoon of sunshine (most of the time, anyway). I went over to my friends to begin setting up, and we started drinking as we were doing so, which must have been around 11 a.m. I wasn't much of a gin drinker, but for some reason, this day, it was my drink of choice, and I was gulping double G&Ts down like they were going out of fashion. It got to the late afternoon, and it was evident that the gin was starting to hit me. I was in a pretty drunken state, but I continued to glug them down.

> "And I wouldn't have blamed them - messy drunk Jess strikes again."

Early evening hits, and everyone is pretty drunk at this point, and things start to get a little out of hand. A few of the girls were having a conversation, which I (out of nowhere) decided to get involved in, and I started shouting at one of my good friends and calling her various mean names. It was as if Jess had disappeared and this horrible, nasty version had replaced her. It got to the point where a few of my other friends decided to step in. I was told to calm down and that maybe I should go home. I then turned my rage onto them before getting up and stumbling out. I'd like to say I went home, but I didn't. I met some other friends in town to continue the night and forget about the impulsive, destructive drama I had just created.

After eventually (somehow) making my way back to my parents' house at around 5 a.m., I woke up in the morning oblivious to what had happened the evening before. I sent a message in our friend's group chat but received no reply from anybody. I didn't think anything of it until one of my friends shortly reached out to ask how I was feeling and if I remembered what had happened.

"I instantly had a huge blanket of dread come over me."

I instantly had a huge blanket of dread come over me. For anybody who is also renowned for being a total mess when under the influence of alcohol, you'll know when somebody asks, "If you remember what happened", it's because nine times out of ten, you've done something stupid. After I was reminded of the previous night's events, it started to slowly come back to me along with the awful things I said to my friend - that part I wish I didn't remember. Words cannot describe how devastating it feels to unintentionally hurt

Phase 0 - Enough is enough

somebody who means so much to you, especially when there is zero truth in the remarks made. I had painted myself in a horrible light, and all I could do was apologise profusely to my friend that I'd hurt in the hope she'd forgive me and know this was entirely out of character. Thankfully, she did forgive me, and we drew a line under the situation; however, she did tell me how hurt the things I'd said had made her feel. It's completely in the past, but if I cast my mind back to this day, I get the same sinking feeling in my stomach as I did back then. I vowed I would never drink gin again after this day - funnily enough, I later discovered that it wasn't just gin that was the "Problem", it was the whole lot. Unfortunately, that was something I had to figure out when the time was right in my journey.

> ## "I get the same sinking feeling in my stomach as I did back then."

There came a point where I needed to have a hard conversation with myself. I could no longer blame others, find excuses or brush off the toxic cycle I was in, and I had to face it head-on and accept that maybe I'm just somebody who isn't able to moderate my drinking, and that's okay. I could never quite understand why others could moderate and I couldn't. Why did I have so little control that I could never go for one drink and have one drink but others could? After endless internal fights with myself, one night finally got the better of me and forced me to face reality. Just over one year ago, I

Phase 0 - Enough is enough

met my partner and some of his friends after work on a Thursday at a local pub for a few drinks. For anybody who lives in London (or a big, vibrant city), you'll know that pubs and bars are usually busy most days of the week; however, they are particularly rammed on Thursdays. I glugged down 4 to 5 beers, which, by that point, meant I was in full "Samantha" mode, as my boyfriend liked to call it (my crazy alter-ego), and I didn't want the night to end. My partner, his brother and I returned to our flat, a short walk from the pub, and the drinks continued. I was drinking whatever I could get my hands on at home to keep my buzz alive. Whisky, wine, vodka, you name it, if it was sat on the bar, I drank it.

"I was drinking whatever I could get my hands on at home, just to keep my buzz alive."

My partner went to sleep not long after we had gotten home. Unlike me, he knew when to call it a night. His brother stayed up a little later with me, and we continued to talk and drink while the drink was still available. My partner's brother then decided to go to bed, but guess what? I wasn't ready to. I had this peculiar habit of being perfectly happy to stay up by myself drinking alone and I think often this was due to not wanting to face the reality of the next day and the hangover that awaited me. Not that staying up later and continuing to drink would minimise this by any means, but my poor, drunk self couldn't quite fathom

Phase 0 - Enough is enough

this and all self-awareness would go entirely out of the window. The next day (when I'd eventually taken myself to bed because the booze had run out), I woke up in a panic, late for work, late for a meeting with my manager and nothing but a huge blanket of shame to cover myself in.

"I was ready to make the change I had been putting off for so long."

After this night, I finally reached my "enough was enough" moment and I was ready to make the change I had been putting off for so long. I no longer wanted to continue this cycle of self-destructive behaviour and knew that somehow, I needed to break it, even though it would likely be one of the hardest things I'd ever have to do. I couldn't let it negatively impact every aspect of my life any longer - I knew deep down I deserved better, and 5-year-old Jess would be so let down. Some people will never understand certain people's relationships with alcohol. They'll often silently judge them for taking it too far and for the lack of self-control they have because they're able to moderate without having this toxic relationship themselves. As I've gotten older and started to understand myself better, I realise part of what made my relationship with alcohol negatively spiral is due to the demons inside of me that I hadn't wanted to face. Alcohol was a great distraction and meant I could put off these issues for a while longer; however, over time, I realised that it was fuelling my problems rather than fixing them, so maybe it was time to let the monsters out of the closet. My "all or nothing" mindset has its positives and negatives. I feel it clashes with alcohol and substances simply for the reason that I never know when to call it a night and when to stop, because I don't want the feeling alcohol gives me to end. Understanding yourself and your characteristics helps build the strength to live a sober life, which we'll get into in detail shortly in the chapters ahead.

"My relationship with alcohol had truly gotten to the point where it had broken me."

Every time I woke up, regretting the night before, was another piece of myself I was slowly tearing apart and letting down. My self-esteem would get less and less to the point that I didn't know how much lower it could get. They say your twenties are the best years of your life, but this couldn't be further from the truth for me. My twenties have mostly been years of self-loathing, anxiety, depression, insecurity and, worst of all, suicidal thoughts. Nothing will ever compare to the feeling that the world would be a better place without you, and I would never wish this feeling on anyone, ever. My relationship with alcohol had truly gotten to the point where it had broken me, and I couldn't get any lower. And when you can't get any lower, the only way is up.

Phase 1
Back to Basics

So you've gotten to the point where you want to make a change and break your ongoing toxic relationship with alcohol, which is amazing. I feel this step is the most important step of them all. The first step in making a change is wanting to make the change, as you cannot help somebody who doesn't want to help themselves.

The fact you're here and reading my book, tells me you've taken this first step and you want to better yourself. I respect you so much for having the hard conversation with yourself, as it's not an easy thing to do or to have to admit. A huge congratulations to you for making it this far already. Now, the key to breaking the cycle is by taking it one step at a time. Nobody who has ever broken up with alcohol has started by telling themselves "I'm going to be sober forever". Yes, this is hopefully your long-term goal, but like anything in life,

Phase 1 - Back to basics

patience is needed, and impactful change doesn't happen overnight. This is a marathon, not a sprint, and it takes time to master. To say you're going to be sober forever is somewhat setting yourself up to fail before you've even started. Similarly to training for a marathon, you wouldn't wake up one day and decide you want to run a marathon the following day (well, you might, and I respect you if you're able to do that), but you would usually prepare a training plan to keep yourself in check and heading in the right direction, to ensure when it gets to race day, you're in the best position you can be to achieve the result you want.

> "This is a marathon, not a sprint, and it takes time to master."

Giving up an addiction or bad habit is very similar to this. You need to become so self-aware that you're prepared for scenarios which might trigger you. Yes, this also comes with experience and being put in uncomfortable situations, however, my intention with this book is to prepare you for what's to come, in the hope it will make your journey to sobriety a little easier.

Firstly, you need to understand your why. What I mean by this is to truly ask yourself what it is about alcohol which makes you turn to it, and is it perhaps used as a distraction to avoid dealing with past, present or future life events which you don't want to face? Asking yourself questions such as "Why do I want to drink?" or

Phase 1 - Back to basics

"Is there something I am trying to escape from when I drink?" will help you to understand why you feel your relationship with alcohol has reached the point where it would be more beneficial if you didn't any longer.

Asking yourself these questions isn't easy, and it might bring up old wounds and emotions that you'd instead be kept buried, or maybe you don't feel you're ready to deal with. One piece of advice I will give you is that you'll feel so much better sitting with yourself and having the hard conversations. You are your own best critic, and this is the utmost act of self-love. We need to keep ourselves in check and hold ourselves accountable when specific behaviour patterns no longer benefit us, the direction we want our lives to go in or the type of person we want to be.

> "We need to keep ourselves in check and hold ourselves accountable when certain behaviour patterns no longer benefit us."

There are many reasons why people turn to alcohol. Some of these include assisting with social situations as a confidence boost, helping to cope with stressful life events, improving our mood, or being a distraction to deal with uncomfortable situations. Yes, some people may also drink for enjoyment; however, I feel anyone who is drinking in excess isn't doing so out of enjoyment, and there is likely something bigger going on deep

Phase 1- Back to basics

down. Next, I'd recommend getting yourself a journal (if you haven't already), and adding journaling to your daily routine to outline your intentions clearly and track your progress. The best thing about journaling is that we consistently check in with ourselves to break down what happened during our day and how it made us feel, so we're in a constant state of reflection. Journaling is a safe space for you and your thoughts to stay in tune. When deciding to make a significant lifestyle change, such as removing alcohol from your life, journaling will help you monitor your progress. This is also a valuable tool for people who want to change their unhealthy relationships with eating or smoking, for example.

> "Journaling is a safe space for you and your thoughts to stay in tune."

Preparing for everything is impossible since life will always throw us curveballs where it feels easier to cope with our emotions by burying them into a bottle of wine than fronting them face on. However, the key is recognising what triggers you, who you're around when you feel triggered, and your emotions at the time. You'll soon discover that there's often a pattern, and you will know what to look out for the next time around. Developing strategies to cope with triggers can help avoid temptation, all whilst getting to know ourselves on a deeper level and doing the necessary shadow

Phase 1 - Back to basics

work. For those unfamiliar with it, shadow work is the process of self-reflecting to uncover the parts of ourselves we often repress and choose to ignore, such as our weaknesses. Shadow work helps us become more self-aware, resulting in more self-acceptance and growth — aspects vital to tackling a toxic relationship with alcohol.

> "Events are often our biggest trigger as we're not prepared for how we're going to feel at the time."

For my next tip, we must start planning. It's all well and good deciding you'd like to remove alcohol from your life, but putting it into action is another challenge altogether. You'll never truly prepare yourself for how you'll feel when you're in the situation when someone offers you a drink at an event, and you say, "No thanks, I don't drink" for the first time, but what we can do is prepare ourselves for those moments in the best way possible. On that note, I want you to write down a list of the events you have coming up, which usually involve drinking. Events are often our biggest trigger, as we're not prepared for how we're going to feel at the time, and this may lead to impulsive drinking and regretting it the following day because you've "Let yourself down again". Don't get me wrong, if this does happen, it doesn't mean you've let yourself down - the furthest thing from it. It just means you have to pick yourself up and try again the next day, keeping in mind what triggered you previously to make you feel like you should or had to turn to alcohol.

Triggering events could be anything from:

- Meeting friends for dinner
- Sports clubs (any excuse for a pint)
- Going to a hen/stag do
- Attending a wedding
- Yours or a loved one's birthday
- Work events
- Holidays or festivals
- Going for afternoon tea (yes, there's usually prosecco involved)
- Date night with partner
- Seasonal holidays (Christmas, New Year's Eve, Easter, Valentine's Day)

And you'll likely think of others to add to the list. You'll notice a pretty obvious pattern with all the events listed above: We can always find a way to involve drinking in almost every aspect of our lives. Bad day at work? A glass of wine. Promotion? A glass of wine. Meeting a friend? A glass of wine. Funeral? A glass of wine…and I'm sure you get the picture.

Alcohol has engrained itself into society to the point where we find events are often strange without it.

Phase 1- Back to basics

And we wonder why it's so difficult to remove it. It's all around us pretty much all of the time. How can you remove something that is always at the forefront of everything? Well, I promise you, you can, and that's what we're here to do - but first, we need to start changing the way you think.

Next, I'd like you to write down all your upcoming events along with the dates so you can start to plan how you will tackle them while ensuring you're still having a great time without feeling triggered. Yes, I know you might think this is a bit excessive, but I promise you, you'll thank me once you're there and realise you already have a plan and feel prepped.

> "I know you might think this is a bit excessive, but I promise you, you'll thank me once you're there."

My next tip would be to cover the details you know about the events, such as how many people are attending and how many people you'll likely know (this plays a huge part in impulsive drinking as if we feel uncomfortable due to not knowing many people, it's easy to turn to alcohol for some booze-fuelled confidence), what you would usually drink at this type of event and what your non-alcoholic, drink of choice is going to be. Replacing alcohol with non-alcoholic alternatives can be a great hack to blending in at big, boozy social scenes. That being said, I appreciate that it isn't a strategy for everyone. I'll usually opt for a 0% beer when I'm in a social setting as it can often avoid me having the same conversation multiple times over about why I'm not drinking and why the person I'm talking to wouldn't say they have a "bad" relationship with alcohol, but they've thought about giving up (heard this one a lot). So I feel this saves me the awkward, unnecessary conversations. However, some people don't like to opt for alcohol-free alternatives and feel this can be a trigger to them then, which results in wanting to later opt for the real thing since the taste is very similar. Your alcohol-free alternative is a personal choice and needs to be a drink or drinks which work well for you. Maybe you'd instead opt for a Coke, coffee or water, which is totally fine, too.

"Your alcohol-free alternative is a personal choice and needs to be a drink or drinks which work well for you."

You may opt for the 0% beer, for example. I'd also recommend that you have a soda or a spritz option in mind, too, just in case the venue doesn't have an alcohol-free alternative and you're then left feeling triggered and put on the spot, so opt for the real thing instead, even though you don't want to. Keeping notes such as this written down in our journal holds us accountable and is a commitment to ourselves to action something, similarly to how a to-do list would

Phase 1 - Back to basics

encourage us to complete tasks, as we hold ourselves responsible to complete them once they're listed and out of our heads.

For example, I attended a summer holiday with the girls, and to make sure I didn't feel triggered, I wrote down in my journal what we were going to be doing during the trip and what my "go-to" alcohol-free drink was going to be, so I had this in my back pocket. I also wrote down an alternative and some notes ahead of the trip. This went something along the lines of…

July 13th-18th - Trip to Ibiza with 10 of the girls

Weds 13th (arrival) dinner and drinks
Drink: Heineken Zero or sparkling water with lemon if they don't have alcohol-free alternatives.

Notes: Likely to result in the girls wanting to go to a club after dinner, as the first night of a holiday is usually pretty full on. Opt to get a taxi back to the hotel if you feel you're not on the same vibe as everybody and don't fancy going to the club. If you do fancy going and are still happy to be out… go!

Benefits: If I don't go, I'll wake up the following day feeling nice and rested and can go for a morning run along the beach. I can then meet the girls after for a nice breakfast before a full day of activities.

Phase 1 - Back to basics

Writing something in a journal like the example I've listed above means you have thought through what could happen but also considered an exit route and the benefits of not falling back into the trap of drinking because you feel you'll miss out on all of the excitement if you don't. Whenever I've thought I could miss out, I'll quickly switch my mind to focus on how great I'll feel the following day, not being hungover, and the things I will be doing or able to do so that I can get excited about that instead. I also considered that the main event of the evening was the welcome dinner, where I got to catch up with good friends I hadn't seen for a while, before everyone got a little drunk and the focus went elsewhere.

> "I'll quickly switch my mind to focus on how great I'll feel the following day not being hungover and the things I will be doing or able to do."

Focus on the positives, and you'll soon realise you haven't missed out. If anything, you've likely dodged a bullet and woke up feeling fresh the next day. Nobody has ever regretted leaving an event early. I know you're with me on that one. You'll also note I've written "if you fancy going, just go" in the above example. Please keep in mind, that this might not be a wise idea if the event is at the beginning of your sobriety journey, as this could trigger you if so. I was nine months into being alcohol-

Phase 1 - Back to basics

free by this point, and had been at triggering events many times before the holiday, so I already knew what feelings to look out for and had some built-up resilience. But you'll notice this didn't stop me from feeling like I needed to prepare for it. This was the first girls' holiday I had been alcohol-free, so I knew it was likely going to feel triggering at times. Journaling before the holiday helped me massively and will likely be something I will continue to do even after one year into my sobriety journey, as there will always be a "first" time you're doing something alcohol-free.

> "There will always be a "first" time you're doing something alcohol-free."

So you've held yourself accountable by listing any events you have coming up which may trigger you to drink again, great - well done you. This means you're now prepped for these scenarios and have thought about how you will navigate them. If you would benefit from support, maybe ask your partner or a close friend to check in with you at the events, even by text if they're not attending, to ensure you're keeping to your plan. Having somebody to hold you accountable and in your corner can be such a great thing. Having someone on the sideline cheering you on and reassuring you that you're making the right decision for you is sometimes the extra little push needed. I do not doubt that you know deep down it is the best thing for you, otherwise

Phase 1 - Back to basics

you wouldn't bother reading this book, but our lack of self-esteem can sometimes try to trick us and convince us otherwise. Sometimes, we need a little extra reassurance. If you do not have a partner or a close friend that you'd feel comfortable asking for this kind of support, I'd recommend signing up for a support group or joining an online community. Many are available and are filled with like-minded individuals in a similar situation to yours.

After all, many years of drinking alcohol can make us lack much confidence, and it's going to take some time to undo many years of making mistakes, embarrassing ourselves, and losing control to the point that we don't even remember what we've done. Our loved ones or a support group stepping in to help support us can be the blessing we didn't know we needed.

"Say good riddance to all the booze because out of sight, out of mind."

The next tip I will give you might seem obvious, but we will cover it anyway, as it might not seem obvious to everybody. As somebody who is trying to remove alcohol from their life, the first place you're going to need to cleanse is your house. Say good riddance to all the booze because *out of sight, out of mind*. If you live with a partner or a friend, I would hope they support you in clearing it from your space, however, if they

Phase 1 - Back to basics

don't, maybe suggest that they keep the alcohol in their private cupboard/room if they still want it available for themselves to drink in the house. I'd be worried if this causes an issue for them - that's very much a "them" problem if it does, not you, and I would hope they would see why this is necessary for you to request and support your decision.

> "You have to train your mind to unlearn the alcohol behaviours indented into you for so long."

Clearing out any undrunk/unopened alcohol from your sacred space means it limits your temptation. If you're constantly reminded of alcohol because it's sat on the bar or drinks trolley in front of you and catching the corner of your eye continually whilst you're watching TV, you're never going to allow yourself to distance it from your mind. It's always going to be there as a reminder. Yes, later on in your sobriety journey, loved ones can add this back into public spaces of the house as you will have built up much more resilience by that point, but for now - say goodbye.

Secondly, I recommend not buying alcohol for others for a while, should they ask you to. We all have those scenarios where we're popping into the shop on our way home and kindly ask our loved ones if they'd like anything or if we're going to a party and stopping to pick up sodas and snacks. Those are the moments where you're likely going to be asked to pick up some alcohol for somebody else. My advice is to apologise and say you're unable to politely. Even make up an excuse if you have to and say that they didn't have the alcohol they asked for in the store. The reason I say this is because your mind is very fragile when trying to break a behavioural habit, and you have to train your mind to unlearn the alcohol behaviours indented into you for so long. With this in mind, we want to avoid making this already challenging process any more difficult for you, so let them pick up their own - I'm sure they're capable of doing so and won't take it personally.

> "You deserve to applaud yourself for the journey you're on."

Last but not least, start keeping a tally of all the consecutive days you've spent alcohol-free. You deserve to applaud yourself for your journey, and keeping count will allow you to see the results coming to life right before your eyes by focusing on it one day at a time. Celebrate the milestones by rewarding yourself with your favourite snack, treat or takeaway. Whether it's one day, one week or one month, it's all worth celebrating, as it's one milestone closer to you becoming the version of yourself you've always wanted to be.

Phase 2
Embrace the loneliness

I wanted to include this next section as I don't feel it's mentioned enough when speaking about the challenges faced when deciding to remove alcohol from our lives and how lonely it can sometimes feel.

The reality is - it can sometimes get pretty lonely, and that's okay. Our loved ones, of course, support us in making positive lifestyle changes; however, this doesn't mean they have to make the same changes themselves, and their relationships with alcohol might be an "okay" one, or they might not feel they want or need to remove it from their lives. This doesn't mean they aren't happy to support you and your decisions. As the weeks pass, you may start to feel a little isolated from stepping away from your usual weekend routines, which often always involve drinking. Whether it's going to the pub on a sunny day and not venturing home until the last

Phase 2- Embrace the loneliness

orders are called, or meeting some friends for dinner and drinks on a Saturday night. Removing alcohol from these situations is bound to feel strange at first. As you change your lifestyle and habits for the better, you might notice yourself unintentionally drifting away from certain friends. Often, this isn't out of choice; however, it's necessary for you and your path, and true friends will stick around to support you through it; that's all that matters.

> "You need to know that you have your own back when times get tough."

Suppose certain loved ones or friends have no desire to give up alcohol and will spend all day drinking, or it's at the forefront of every activity you do together. How can you continue to spend time with them unless they're able to try something new without revolving it around alcohol? I keep referring back to self-love, and you'll notice I do a lot throughout this book, as it is the most essential tool when opting for a life of sobriety. You need to know that you have your own back when times get tough, and you're not going to revert to old ways because you have a moment of weakness and worry that you're friends aren't going to like you or invite you to events because you're "no longer fun" in their eyes. The reality is, if your friends decide to exclude you from things or don't want to mix up what you do together to make sure alcohol isn't the centre of it, then maybe it's

Phase 2 - Embrace the loneliness

time to question if they're true friends and if they have your back. I'd also recommend that those friends read this book as if alcohol means that much to them and they don't want to bond with you without it; I think it's time they have one of the hard conversations with themselves mentioned in the previous chapter.

For a while, you might need to distance yourself from places such as the pub, festivals or events so you can break the cycle and your relationship with those places when it comes to alcohol, as they're familiar drinking environments. Don't get me wrong, if you have a wedding coming up, for example, then of course I don't expect you not to attend. But yes, it's going to be tricky for you to navigate alongside your newfound sobriety than, say, if you had a wedding one year into this journey.

> "You'll wake up feeling so liberated and proud the following day.

If you have a wedding, for example, if you've followed the journaling tips mentioned in the previous chapter and have a loved one checking in with you, you'll do great. You'll wake up feeling so liberated and proud the following day, knowing you stayed true to yourself and didn't cave under pressure. Distancing yourself means precisely what it says - it's just distance. It doesn't mean you can never revisit these places, it just means

Phase 2 - Embrace the loneliness

you need some separation for a while to figure out what the new you aside from alcohol looks like. If you had asked me two years ago if I ever envisioned myself sitting in a pub, drinking a 0% beer or a soda and lime, I probably would've laughed and said no way am I capable of sitting there without drinking alcohol, but still having a good time. But now, I'll happily go to the same pubs I got absolutely wasted in and sit there with my 0% or soda and not think about alcohol once. If I can get here, trust me, you can too. But first, you need to allow yourself time to adjust by stepping away from specific environments for a while.

> "Now you've stopped drinking, you suddenly have so much more time on your hands to try the things you've always wanted to do... hangover-free!"

Consider taking up a new hobby, as it's a great way to meet new, like-minded people whilst also taking your mind off the recent changes to your routine, and guess what? Now that you've stopped drinking, you suddenly have so much more time on your hands to try the things you've always wanted to do... hangover-free! Perhaps you want to work on your fitness; well, use this time to your advantage, as exercising is a fantastic distraction that benefits every aspect of our health for the better. I found that giving up alcohol and improving my fitness went hand in hand, and I suddenly became really into

Phase 2 - Embrace the loneliness

running. Running is a great way to exercise and is amazing for our mental health. This was an excellent way for me to feel good, work on my fitness, and distract myself by setting distance or pace targets to achieve. Instead of going to the pub on a Friday night, I would go for a long run whilst listening to a podcast and felt equally as good, if not better, for doing so. This also meant I could treat myself to whatever carb-filled Friday night dinner I had in mind and sweet treats, guilt-free. I appreciate that running is not for everybody, so don't feel this is a hobby you have to make work for you. There are plenty of other hobbies to try, which are a great way to spend time, meet new people and learn new skills.

Some include:

- Join a book club
- Get a gym membership
- Joining a dance or fitness club
- Walking Group
- Volunteering
- Language class
- Cinema club
- Cooking class
- Painting or Pottery class

And I'm sure you'll think of some others too.

Phase 2 - Embrace the loneliness

We've touched on the fact that if friends aren't supporting you through your sobriety journey, they may not be your real friends. However, it's also worth adding that we can sometimes force certain relationships to end and self-sabotage ourselves during this phase of figuring out our "New normal."

We often assume people won't want to hang out with us anymore and already create an image of what we think others must be thinking about us, which, nine times out of ten, isn't the case at all.

> "The fact is, you'll never know unless you try."

Something I found particularly challenging during the first couple of months of sobriety was facing the fact that perhaps some of my friendships had been formed on drunken nights out, and I was scared to find out if we had a friendship outside of that. "What if they think I'm boring?" or "What if we have nothing in common?" were common self-sabotaging questions I had to shut down often in the early stages.

The fact is, you'll never know unless you try. Yes, it might feel slightly uncomfortable not having alcohol as your safety blanket—but what I do know is you are far more fun and exciting without it, and I don't even need to meet you to know that. You don't need alcohol to make you seem more interesting than you already are.

Phase 2 - Embrace the Loneliness

Just be you, and the right people will gravitate in time. If you find certain relationships do naturally end because you've drifted apart and no longer have anything in common, your future self will thank you for this one day, as you've put yourself and your needs above pleasing others, which is no easy thing to do. The right people will also come along as you're reinventing yourself, I promise - so hang tight and make sure you're your main focus in the meantime.

> "It was my safe space to listen to individuals who shared similar experiences."

During my first month of sobriety, I found much comfort in listening to relatable podcasts. It was my safe space to listen to individuals who shared similar experiences to me when it came to alcohol and who also shared similar views on how choosing sobriety can sometimes feel a little isolating, especially at first. It felt like a constant reminder that my decision was the right one as, at first, it's normal to question yourself because you don't have many people around you that you can talk to about it, which is often just our lack of self-esteem talking.

My absolute favourite (for anybody who likes to listen to podcasts or feels this could be a useful option for them during their journey) is "How I quit alcohol" by Australian host Danni Carr. This show, in particular,

Phase 2 - Embrace the loneliness

resonated with me on a deeper level, more so than others, as Danni would have guests on the podcast from all walks of life at different life stages and backgrounds. I loved listening to guests in their twenties talking about sobriety, as I didn't really know anybody my age who experienced similar issues to me when it came to alcohol who had also decided it was no longer benefiting them. After further research, I discovered many groups you can join designed for sober or sober-curious people. However, this wasn't something I had thought to look into at the time.

"So many positives can come from outgrowing a familiar environment."

It can be very isolating at first breaking up with alcohol. I would be lying to you if I said that sometimes it doesn't make us feel great to feel a little out of place in places that have been so familiar for such a long time. Still, it can also be unique, and many positives can come from outgrowing a familiar environment. We often get stuck in cycles that no longer serve us, but we don't know where to start in making the change. Well, you've decided you want to make this change, and embracing the loneliness can be very empowering.

You've decided that you're ready for the change, and you're now ready to get to know yourself without

Phase 2- Embrace the loneliness

alcohol, try new things and go to new places. We only get one life, and there's no do-over. Taking a break from the local pub to try out a book club, for example, isn't a waste of time, and you'll likely find that you wish you'd tried it sooner.

Alternatively, you might find that opting for an evening alone once in a while with a bubble bath (yes men, I'm talking to you too!), a good book, a sweet treat and your phone on do not disturb is just what your mind and body needs after a long, stressful week at the office.

Phase 3
Rediscovery - Date yourself

When I say date yourself...I genuinely mean it! It's the best way to get to know yourself, what you want out of life, and who you want to be. Dating yourself is all about regaining the respect and confidence within you that alcohol might have taken away or damaged over time. It can help you to discover more about your interests, desires, likes and dislikes, and help you achieve your goals and fulfil your true potential - all without alcohol being the centre of everything and holding you back in achieving the things you want from your life.

Being comfortable in your skin is so important and can improve all aspects of your life in one way or another. Spending time alone can help us deal with conflicts better as we know ourselves on a deeper level, which

Phase 3- Rediscovery - Date yourself

can only benefit our relationships within ourselves, with our colleagues, friends, partners, and loved ones.

In the last chapter, we covered that early sobriety can be a little lonely, but it can also allow us to get to know ourselves again as we step into this next chapter of our lives. Removing alcohol means we get to see the world differently. We no longer have this dark, negative cloud looming over us, and we can start to see just how many possibilities there are out there waiting for us without using alcohol as a distraction. The world is our oyster, and we no longer have this persistent barrier blocking our way. With that being said, it's time for you to get to know yourself again and start rebuilding the self-love that alcohol has likely broken down over time. It's time to be a boss!

> "The world is our oyster, and we no longer have this persistent barrier blocking our way."

Everyone's level of self-confidence is different, so I appreciate that you might be reading this and feeling that lack of self-confidence isn't something that has ever been an issue for you or needs working on. I can only speak from my personal experience and how I feel alcohol has affected me and taken its toll. I hope you, as readers, can also relate to this and find comfort in knowing that you are not alone. If you feel you're ready to part ways with alcohol then the likelihood is that it

Phase 3 - Rediscovery - Date yourself

has damaged you in some way and has made you feel somewhat insecure, likely from various events which might have happened whilst being under the influence of alcohol, big or small.

I've found that intentionally spending more time alone has allowed me to get to know myself more deeply. It's allowed me to become more self-aware of not only my strengths but my weaknesses and has given me the time to work on them both without using alcohol as a distraction. I've started to enjoy my own company and have become very aware of how valuable my time is, how I choose to spend it and who I spend it with. I've grown to like who I'm becoming without needing to rely on alcohol for a confidence boost. You can't hate yourself into change; this comes from finding the love within, knowing you deserve more, and being ready to do whatever it takes for your happiness.

> "I've started to enjoy my own company and have become very aware of how valuable my time is."

Never in a million years would I have found the confidence to write this book whilst still drinking alcohol. I've always wanted to write and love it, but I have never had the self-discipline to do so and would always make excuses or feel that I didn't have the time.

Phase 3 - Rediscovery - Date yourself

That being said, I'd always manage to find the time for the pub...It's funny how our priorities change, right? I hope I can be the living proof you need that removing alcohol from your life means you can find the confidence to complete your goals and aspirations, whatever they might be. You are worthy of great things and must have faith in yourself, know what's best for you, and trust in the process.

> "Doing uncomfortable things is usually the most rewarding."

Now...for the fun stuff. When we say date ourselves, what does this involve? It means you need to prioritise time for yourself and your needs. Over time, how you show this to yourself will become clear. If you spend little time alone, then it might feel like an odd concept at first. Taking yourself on a solo date can push you out of your comfort zone, but doing uncomfortable things is usually the most rewarding. Trying new things and venturing alone can nudge you to dive into experiences you've never considered. For those in relationships, you can go on self-dates, too. In fact, I strongly encourage it! Don't get me wrong, I'm not a relationship expert, but I know that taking time for yourself whilst in a relationship shows respect for yourself and your independence, aside from your partner and outside of the relationship. I hope they'll also appreciate you

Phase 3 - Rediscovery - Date yourself

taking this time for yourself whilst getting to know yourself and your newfound sobriety. In fact, I hope they admire you for it, because I certainly do!

There are so many ways to treat ourselves to solo date days/nights, or even solo holidays. I've listed some of these below so you can start planning.

Have you thought about taking yourself:

- Shopping
- For coffee and cake (obviously)
- To a movie
- On a tourist day (within or outside of your town/city)
- To a food/local market
- On a hike/long walk
- To a cooking class
- To a comedy night
- For lunch or dinner (and yes, get dressed up!)
- On a staycation
- To a spa day/weekend
- For a picnic with your favourite book
- To watch a sunset
- To watch a play/show
- On a bike ride
- On holiday - start ticking off those bucket list destinations.

A solo date can also include a night in. Nothing screams self-love more than pampering yourself, putting on

Phase 3 - Rediscovery - Date yourself

your favourite film/series, listening to your favourite playlist or podcast, enjoying your favourite food and putting your phone on Do Not Disturb. What we want to achieve from dating ourselves is to get to know who we are and our behaviours. Spending time alone helps us begin to understand ourselves without alcohol, which is a huge distraction. Having exceptional self-awareness is one of the most critical factors in living a sober life. To be self-aware, you need to know yourself better than anybody else. You're probably thinking, how can I not know myself when I spend every day within my mind and body? The reality is, the majority of people don't know themselves on a deeper level. They know what they like and dislike but don't know anything more profound than that, and aren't willing to do the work to find out. Knowing ourselves on a deeper level allows us to recognise when we are feeling triggered and enables us to change specific behaviour patterns without relying on the famous "Willpower" to step in for us because, let's face it, it rarely does.

> "Knowing ourselves on a deeper level allows us to recognise when we are feeling triggered."

We've touched on journaling in the previous chapters, which also plays a massive part in self-discovery. Not only are journals a good tool for planning, but they're also a great escape from everyday life by clearing our heads of negative thoughts and putting them onto paper. They're also a fantastic tool to get to know

Phase 3 - Rediscovery - Date yourself

ourselves and try to understand who we are on a deeper level. All it takes is for you to put aside 10 minutes every morning or evening to check in with yourself and your sobriety journey. I've written some questions below, which are a great starting point. There are both light-hearted and more profound questions for you to begin answering when you feel ready. These can be altered slightly depending on whether you answer them in the morning before your day starts or during the evening when you're reflecting.

Light-hearted Questions

1. How am I feeling today?
2. What day into my sobriety journey am I on?
3. What am I enjoying about my sobriety journey so far?
4. What am I struggling with in my sobriety journey so far?
5. What did I achieve today, or what would I like to achieve?
6. What will I do to relax/enjoy myself today?
7. What is one thing I've done or will do today to support my future self?
8. What are three things I am grateful for and why?
9. Did anything trigger me today and how did I deal with it/overcome it, or what might trigger me today?
10. How can I make today/tomorrow better?

Phase 3 - Rediscovery - Date yourself

Deeper Questions

1. What emotions or feelings do I experience that lead me to want to drink alcohol?
2. How does drinking affect my relationships with others?
3. What role does alcohol play in my life?
4. Am I using alcohol as a coping mechanism, and if so, why do I think that is?
5. How do I feel about my drinking habits?
6. How would my life change if I removed alcohol from my routine?
7. What are my long-term goals, and how does drinking align with them?
8. What am I trying to run away from whilst drinking?
9. What are some things I possibly haven't dealt with in the past, and how can I start to deal with them today without alcohol being used as a distraction?
10. Why do I think I drink, and what do I enjoy about drinking? Equally, what scares me about not drinking?

You may think of some others you'd like to ask yourself too, which is great. The more self-discovery questions you can answer, the better your self-discovery will be. I should also mention that the deeper questions can be challenging to answer in one sitting, so be patient with yourself. There's no rush, and this is your journey.

Phase 4
The healthy stuff

There are so many benefits to giving up alcohol, and it would be wrong for us not to cover them in this book, as the facts speak for themselves. Yes, socially, alcohol can be a difficult mechanism to escape. Still, it's way easier to leave something behind when you realise how toxic it's being to your mind and body and how better off you will find yourself overall without it. In this chapter, we will break down the various benefits and the reasons why it's so harmful. I hope by the time you finish this chapter, you feel enlightened, as it really can be eye-opening to learn just how many benefits there are from giving up alcohol. Some benefits have been proven to be visible in as little as one week of not drinking…crazy, right? Quitting or taking a break is all our body needs to start repairing itself.

Phase 4- The healthy stuff

Better Quality of Sleep and More Energy

From the moment you rule alcohol out of your life completely, one of the first things you can expect is your energy levels to increase, and you'll suddenly stop feeling fatigued and sluggish. This is often the result of having better-quality sleep. The quality of our sleep will affect almost everything throughout our day-to-day lives without us even realising it.

How often have you rolled into bed at 4 am to wake up feeling exhausted and heavily sleep deprived, even though you woke up at say, midday, so still managed to get 8 hours of sleep? Well, you may have had 8 hours of sleep, but this was by no means the restful, deep sleep your body needs. Or perhaps you've been out day drinking and are thinking, "Great, I can get into bed at a reasonable time, and wake up feeling fresh," yet you never seem to wake up feeling all that fresh, even with an early night? Alcohol acts as a barrier and means we spend less time in the rapid eye movement (REM) cycle of sleep. This is the deepest part of our sleep and has the most restorative effect on our body. Disruptions to REM sleep can affect our mood, memory, and cognitive function.

"Sleep quality will affect almost everything throughout our day-to-day lives."

Since alcohol acts as a depressant to our central nervous system, it can slow down our brain activity, making us feel relaxed or sleepy, regardless of whether we've had the entire 7-9 hours we should have. This often makes people believe that alcohol helps to improve sleep, so having a glass of wine every night after work allows us to relax and start to feel drowsy. Yes, alcohol can seem as though it is helping us to relax, and you might fall asleep quicker, but in reality, drinking before bedtime puts you at risk of experiencing repeated awakenings and low-quality sleep later in the night. This means the quality of the sleep you're experiencing is very low. Regular or heavy drinking can also contribute to the development of insomnia. Insomnia is a sleep disorder many people have, which means they find it difficult to fall asleep and stay asleep. As many as three-quarters of people with

Phase 4 - The healthy stuff

alcohol dependence experience symptoms of insomnia when they drink, which can worsen over time. According to the National Institute of Health (NIH), sleep deficient individuals are less productive at work and school. They take longer to finish tasks, react slower, and make more mistakes. Now, I can't speak for you, but I can say from my own experiences with alcohol and how exhausted I would feel not just the following day after heavily drinking, but up to three days after. I felt like my body was always trying to recover and I never felt rested. By the time I got back on track, the cycle would start all over again as the weekend would be in near the distance, meaning I often felt fatigued, exhausted, and lacked concentration since I always felt tired.

> ## "I often felt fatigued, exhausted and lacked concentration."

Did you know that as little as one alcoholic drink can affect your quality of sleep? So, imagine how much binge drinking can take its toll. It's been proven that just having one alcoholic drink can affect your sleep quality (yes, one!) by approximately 9%. If this is the case for just one drink, imagine how much damage ten drinks will do. A 2018 Finnish study found that any amount of alcohol consumed before bed can hurt sleep quality, with low amounts decreasing it by over 9% and high amounts by almost 40%. Alcohol can make it easier to fall asleep at first, but the effects wear off

Phase 4 - The healthy stuff

after a few hours, as your body tries to eliminate it. Deep sleep, also known as NREM (Non-rapid eye movement) Stage three sleep, is essential for repairing the body and clearing waste from the brain. Whilst we're asleep, our body starts to reset itself, and alcohol can act as a barrier during the process as our brains then focus on removing the alcohol in the first instance, before assuming its ordinary course of action. Not getting enough deep sleep can affect our immune system and may increase our risk for dementia and chronic diseases such as Cancer. We've covered the adverse effects alcohol has on our sleep, and now let's cover the benefits. We'll cover many of the benefits listed below shortly in more detail, but as far as our sleep is concerned, having quality sleep has a fantastic amount of health benefits.

These include:

- **Physical health:** Quality sleep has been convincingly tied to a healthier body (both inside and out), a better immune response, and a longer life. Restful sleep helps us maintain a healthy weight, improves our heart health, and can lower our risk of chronic conditions like diabetes and strokes. It can also help us get sick less often and support our immune system.

- **Mental health:** Quality sleep can help reduce stress, improve our mood, and get along better with

Phase 4 - The healthy stuff

people. It can also help us think more clearly, form long-term memories, and improve in school and work. Allowing our minds to rest can increase our capacity for self-awareness, empathy, and moral judgments. Our brains consolidate and organise memories during deep sleep, which can help us process more clearly what we learned the previous day.

- **Brain function:** Quality sleep can improve our brain performance and attention span, including learning and memory. Sleep helps form new neural pathways that will enhance learning and memory. It also helps to improve our emotional well-being.

- **Growth and stress hormones:** Quality sleep can affect our growth and stress hormones, such as reducing cortisol levels. Cortisol is a stress hormone responsible for our body's fight-or-flight response. A lack of sleep can cause the body to release more cortisol, increasing stress and anxiety. Sleep improves our growth hormone levels, which are important for cell growth and repair. Growth hormone levels are highest during the first few hours of sleep, especially deep sleep.

- **Blood pressure:** Quality sleep can positively affect our blood pressure and help it decrease. Studies have found that even a small drop in blood pressure can reduce the risk of heart attack by up to 10%.

- **Metabolism:** Quality sleep can help improve our metabolism by impacting appetite and regulating ghrelin and leptin levels, the hormones that signal hunger and satisfaction. Sleep deprivation can cause ghrelin levels to rise and leptin levels to fall, which can lead to overeating.

Sleep is one of the most vital factors to the body. Deep, meaningful sleep is how our body resets and repairs itself and fights off disease and infection. Alcohol has a substantial negative influence on restful sleep, with all of the above factors likely to be influenced by frequent binges and nights of disrupted sleep. Having a healthy sleep pattern is crucial to our overall health and well-being.

Phase 4 - The healthy stuff

Weight loss and maintaining a healthy weight

Speaking from experience, I noticed a positive change in my weight pretty quickly after removing alcohol from my diet. And yes, I include alcohol when talking about diet, as sometimes there are more calories in the drinks we consume than there are in the food we eat. I wouldn't necessarily say I was overweight. However, I knew losing a few pounds would only benefit me. I'd also tried many diets in the past, which never worked, as I would give up after a few weeks of seeing no results - of course, no matter how much I dieted, I would never think to remove alcohol, which is the reason I would never see results. Diets never work anyway, but that's a conversation for a different book! Without trying, I lost a few pounds within the first 3-4 weeks of giving up the *booze*. This was purely

Phase 4- The healthy stuff

unintentional and I would still treat myself to snacks when I felt like it. This was down to several reasons, the first being that once I gave up drinking, I started exercising more frequently and enjoyed the high I would get from running. It was almost as if I'd replaced the pub with running, and I was starting to see the benefits.

"It was almost as if I'd replaced the pub with running, and I was starting to see the benefits."

The likelihood is that if you've tried to go on various diets and have seen no results, it's because you've never removed alcohol from the equation. Many people aren't aware of just how many empty calories there are in alcoholic drinks, and the fact that it's often never just the one drink consumed means the calories rack up pretty quickly without us even knowing, resulting in unintentional weight gain.

The next section of this book might be pretty eye-opening for some of you regarding how many calories there are in alcoholic drinks, as it certainly was for me. The good news is that you're reading this book because you already know you want to cut your ties with alcohol, and you didn't need me to assist you in getting here. The information covered within this book is to guide and reassure you that you're making the right decision for you and your life, and there are so many

Phase 4 - The healthy stuff

positives to come from it. Did you know a standard glass of wine can contain up to 158 calories, with a large glass containing approximately 228, and some pints of stronger lager containing up to 222 calories? These are broad units of measure and will vary slightly depending on the brand and type, but this is to give you a baseline understanding. So, the bottle of wine you might be consuming whilst alone, with your partner, or out with friends could be adding 800 or so calories onto your daily calorie intake without you even realising it. And that's just one bottle per night.

> *"Yet you often wonder why you're not seeing the results from consistent exercise and altering your eating habits."*

What if this scenario occurs two to three times per week? I'll let you do the math. The 2-3 beers you're having in the evenings each night or maybe every other night? Well, that's an extra 600 calories sometimes, yet you often wonder why you're not seeing the results from consistent exercise and altering your eating habits. Yes, we've all sadly been there. Wine and Beer are the worst offenders and contain the most calories, with spirits tending to rank lower on the list. Much to my surprise, Cocktails are a close third on the list. Yes, I hate to say it, but just because they're often mixed with fruit juice doesn't mean they provide us with any real nutritional benefit. One margarita or daiquiri can contain up to 35 grams of sugar, with the maximum daily sugar intake for men being 36 grams and for women no more than 25 grams per day. By having just one cocktail, you've reached or gone over this limit already, and let's be honest, it's never just the one margarita…Bars invented two-for-one cocktails for a reason, but it wasn't to benefit our health.

> "Any form of healthy eating habits I had would go straight out of the window as soon as a hangover reared its ugly head."

Yes, there are many hidden calories in alcoholic drinks, but that's not the only thing which adds to unintentional weight gain. I don't know about you, but from experience, any form of healthy eating habits I had would go straight out of the window as soon as a hangover reared its ugly head. Because I often had hangovers which wouldn't allow me to eat without throwing the food straight back up, I rarely ate during the day if I was severely hungover, but when this phase passed, I would eat anything and everything I could get my hands on. When hungover, we're drawn to terrible food because our bodies need immediate fuel. Our brains feel the best way to refuel is to target foods heavier in calories, such as greasy foods, carbs and sugar. Our body particularly likes Glycogen to fuel itself, so when we use our glycogen stores to metabolise alcohol, our body demands us to give it more by making us feel super hungry. Consuming a considerable amount of alcohol also reduces the levels of anti-diuretic hormone (ADH) in the bloodstream. When there's less ADH in our blood, our kidneys do not reabsorb as much water, resulting in our bodies producing more urine. This is why we're highly dehydrated the morning after drinking alcohol. Dehydration is another reason we want salty/greasy foods, so when all of this is considered, it's obvious why we crave unhealthy takeaways when hungover - our body is crying out for a way to refuel itself quickly and enters a form of survival mode. Ironically, being sober has drastically decreased my cravings for "bad" food. I find I rarely have the urge to eat takeaways or junk food since taking alcohol out of the equation.

> "Our body is crying out for a way to refuel itself quickly and enters a form of survival mode."

Unhealthy, greasy foods are addictive, similar to alcohol. Therefore, our bodies remember the feeling and recognise that we often consume it whilst hungover, so it puts two and two together. If we take away alcohol for some time, our bodies start to forget the taste/impact junk food gives us too, and we no longer crave it since it's being replaced with a healthier, balanced diet which provides way more nutrients than

Phase 4 - The healthy stuff

1-3 takeaways per week ever could. I can also vouch that the same applies to giving up alcohol. After a while, you suddenly don't miss it and have no desire or craving for it. The "I need a glass of wine" feeling gradually leaves your body, and good riddance to it at that. Do you remember your first sip of alcohol and how you thought it was awful (or at least I did), yet continued to try it over and over again until you eventually started to like it? The good news is that this process works in reverse, too, and the mind is great at forgetting the taste of things if the body is withdrawn from it over time. I will mention this in no way, shape, or form is me telling you that you have to give up alcohol and junk food at the same time. This is me speaking from my own experience, and I found I no longer craved the food I would crave previously, often whilst hungover, from a night of heavy drinking.

"Once you've mastered your sobriety journey, you can look to improve other aspects of your life."

Everyone's journey is different, and you might find that this isn't the case for you. If you find you still want to consume junk food or have takeaways, then go for it. Quitting alcohol is a huge step forward for yourself, and focusing on this and only this for a period I'm confident is enough to help your weight decrease by

Phase 4 - The healthy stuff

itself, alongside any junk food, as you remove the empty calories from all the alcohol, as outlined above.

Once you've mastered your sobriety journey, you can then look to improve other aspects of your life, should you wish to, which may or may not involve improving your diet. Giving up alcohol is challenging, and we deserve to reward ourselves for the strength we're putting into improving our lives. If this means having a sweet treat or a takeaway when you want it, then so be it. My guilty pleasure has always been sweet treats, so naturally, I crave sweets and ice cream. When I first gave up alcohol, I found I wanted to treat myself to snacks more occasionally because it was filling the void that alcohol used to fill. Over time, this naturally disappeared as I became passionate about running and improving other aspects of my life. This isn't to say I won't treat myself to an ice cream or a pack of Haribo's at present if I want them because I most certainly will.

"Many people often try to fill a void in their lives with alcohol."

The key thing to remember is that most addictions start with us and are a result of the things we aren't dealing with deep within. I turned to junk food for some time after quitting alcohol because as I mentioned above, it filled a void I used to fill with alcohol. But then I started to ask myself why I felt the need to "Fill a void" at all.

Phase 4 - The healthy stuff

It was because I felt empty, and specific aspects of my life weren't fulfilling. I'd turn to alcohol as a distraction and thrived from the chaos for a while, as it meant I didn't have to face my feelings front on - I could continue kicking the can down the road.

Many people often try to fill a void in their lives with alcohol, food, relationships, work, and things that are supposed to distract our attention. It means we don't have to do the hard work and have the conversations with ourselves we know we should be having but do everything in our power not to have.

Phase 4 - The healthy stuff

Skin Improvement

It's often said that you can tell how healthy a person is from their overall complexion. The skin is known to be the largest organ in our body, so there's really no hiding it if our skin starts to show signs of, let's say, "Wear and tear" from addictions or alcohol abuse.

I was surprisingly very aware, whilst drinking alcohol frequently, of the effect it was having on my skin, and I knew my skin never looked great whilst hungover. It looked exactly as I often felt - exhausted, dull and crying out for some love and attention. There was no hiding my dark circles from the lack of quality sleep or the dryness from my poor dehydrated body, and people were quick to tell me that "I looked tired", which we all know is just a nice way of telling somebody that they look like crap. I'd look as though the nutrients had been

Phase 4 - The healthy stuff

totally stripped from my body, and this was likely the case since I'd usually been spending most of the day throwing up. Well, the great news is, as soon as you stop drinking alcohol, the effects reverse themselves over time and you'll begin to see a positive change in your overall complexion. Alcohol dehydrates and can lead to dull, dry skin, resulting in a loss of fluid and nutrients essential for healthy-looking skin.

> "Alcohol dehydrates and can lead to dull, dry skin, resulting in a loss of fluid and nutrients essential for healthy looking skin."

Over time, excessive alcohol can make our skin look grey, dull, wrinkled, swollen and puffy. Other side effects of dehydration include sunken eyes, dry lips and accelerated ageing. Excessive use of alcohol can also have some long-term effects on the skin, such as an increased risk of skin infections and bacterial and fungal infections. These are more likely to occur if you drink excessively since alcohol weakens your immune system and damages the ability of your body to absorb nutrients. Ironically, the more alcohol we drink, even though it's a fluid, the more dehydrated our bodies become. I'm sure you've noticed the "red flush" some people get after as little as one drink, or you might even be a victim of this yourself. Putting it simply, Alcohol releases a histamine that dilates the blood's

Phase 4- The healthy stuff

capillaries, resulting in redness of the skin. It's possible that over several years and persistent drinking, this inflammation and redness can remain permanent. Now, if drinking can have this effect on our skin, imagine the effect it has on our insides. While the flushing itself isn't considered harmful, it could be a warning sign of other risks. Some studies showed that people who get flushed after drinking may have a higher chance of developing high blood pressure.

"Giving our bodies a break from drinking allows the skin to rehydrate and regenerate."

It's no secret that Alcohol can also aid acne in all ages since it dilates the pores of the skin, leading to a higher chance of getting blackheads. It can also be the cause of hormonal imbalances that lead to acne. Alcohol overstimulates the sebaceous glands, which produce sebum (an oily, waxy substance that helps protect and moisturise the skin and hair). Excess sebum can mix with dead skin cells and bacteria in pores, creating new spots. It can also aggravate existing breakouts. Giving our bodies a break from drinking allows the skin to rehydrate and regenerate. I started noticing changes in my skin after just a couple of weeks and quickly noticed that my skin felt more dewy and healthier. This coincides with getting better quality sleep, which resulted in my dark circles looking less prominent and

Phase 4 - The healthy stuff

eating healthier since I minimised the amount of takeaways and junk food I ate due to being hungover. Don't get me wrong, it's a privilege to get to age, and I do believe we should all age gracefully; however, if there was a way to slow down the ageing process, wouldn't you want to know what it was? Now, there's no scientifically proven way to stop ageing, but wouldn't you grab onto it with both hands if you found a way to look and feel younger? Removing alcohol from your life is certainly a great place to start, and many people appear to have a younger appearance once they choose a life of sobriety. A key reason for this is that once alcohol is removed from the equation, our skin is more equipped to retain moisture, resulting in a more hydrated, radiant and fresher complexion. It's also proven to reduce the appearance of fine lines and wrinkles, one of the key signs of ageing.

Phase 4 - The healthy stuff

**Risk of Disease and
Bodily Damage Decreases**

Speaking about disease can be super challenging, as the likelihood is you know somebody or potentially are an individual who has experienced what disease can do and how truly devastating it can be if it's not treatable. Yes, I will say there are many diseases out there which are totally out of our control, and we have to count our lucky stars that we and our loved ones don't happen to get one, or if we do, it's treatable. But, there are also some diseases we can minimise our risk of getting and the overall damage to our bodies just by removing alcohol from our lives. Several studies show that if you stop drinking, your chances of getting cancer, having a stroke and early death are likely to decrease. One thing I do know for sure is that disease opens up our eyes as to how short life can be and that we should make every

Phase 4 - The healthy stuff

single moment count, as we never know when it will be our last. The fact that the link between disease and alcohol isn't spoken about more truly amazes me. Why isn't something that can be so detrimental to our health in many ways not publicised? Why isn't there more of a surge to make this known on a larger scale? I could sit here explaining why I feel we aren't made aware of this more. The reality is that we're here to run through some of the hard truths and why quitting alcohol decreases our chances of getting certain diseases in so many ways and improves the overall functioning of our bodies.

> "Why isn't something which can be so detrimental to our health in many ways not publicised? Why isn't there more of a surge to make this known on a larger scale?"

Remember that all that matters is that we are doing the best we can for ourselves and our health with the information we have, but we have to make sure we're actively searching for the information as it's sadly rarely given to us. How can you even begin to improve your health if you don't know where to start or what damage alcohol is potentially causing? I apologise in advance if the next section is uncomfortable, however, I feel I wouldn't be doing my part in providing you with all the facts if I didn't include it. The harsh reality is that you need to know this, and if you're anything like me,

Phase 4- The healthy stuff

this will very likely prevent you from wanting to drink ever again. I don't believe the small satisfactions we get from drinking are worth the long-term damage it causes or could potentially cause, and I hope you agree, but I shall leave that up to you to decide for yourself. Almost every part of the body is affected by alcohol. When a person drinks, alcohol heads to the stomach, where some of it is absorbed, and the liver then processes it. Alcohol then moves through the brain, the heart and the kidneys. Alcohol in our blood also passes through our lungs.

"Almost every part of the body is affected by alcohol."

According to Medical Reviewer Ashraf Ali, "each part of the body experiences short and long-term effects of alcohol. Our organs recover from the short-term side effects in hours or days, but they don't recover from the long-term effects. This damage gets worse each time we drink. The risks of permanent damage are also increased when a person is mixing drugs and alcohol." I hate to say it, but there are so many parts of the body negatively impacted by alcohol, and this gave me a huge wake-up call. With this in mind, I've summarised some of the facts I feel are valuable for you to know below.

Phase 4 - The healthy stuff

Brain

We've all experienced the short-term effects of drinking on our brains in one form or another, such as slurred speech, blurred vision, impaired memory, lack of coordination and, in some cases, mood swings - but what are the long-term effects? Long-term effects can or may include:

- **Neurotoxicity:** Neurotoxicity is the damage to the central nervous system that can occur from exposure to toxic substances such as alcohol, which, over time, damages our brain cells. Long-term heavy drinking can also lead to brain shrinkage, particularly in regions such as the frontal lobe (the area responsible for various functions related to higher cognitive abilities and social skills), limbic system (group of interconnected brain structures that play a crucial role in regulating our emotions, memory processing, and behaviours) and cerebellum (a small but vital part of our brain that helps coordinate and regulate many functions and processes).

- **Shrinking:** Heavy alcohol consumption per day is associated with the most significant risk for brain shrinkage. Even drinking just one drink per day may reduce brain volume. Drinking four units of alcohol a day can potentially cause structural damage and

Phase 4- The healthy stuff

brain volume loss equivalent to 10 years of ageing...yes, 10 years.

- **Cognitive and memory problems:** Over time, frequent alcohol consumption can impact our memory, with many individuals finding they're unable to remember directions to familiar places, have trouble remembering appointments or recalling what they've just done or should be doing. It can also lead to unexpected confusion, with many people struggling with an everyday task or experiencing frequent brain fog. This is because alcohol slows down how nerves communicate in a part of the brain called the hippocampus, which is the region that plays a significant role in helping people form and maintain memories. Consuming alcohol to excess can often lead to blackouts and periods where you cannot remember what happened. Various factors which influence the deterioration of memory include the amount of alcohol intake and its frequency, the age at which the person started to consume alcohol, family history of alcoholism, the basic demographics of an individual, and whether the individual was exposed to alcohol in the womb...crazy, right? According to the Alzheimer's Organisation, a study found that while moderate consumption was linked to a slight decrease in Alzheimer's disease, regular over-consumption of alcohol increases the risk of developing Alzheimer's disease by a staggering 300%.

Liver

Many people are aware that one of the main organs affected by alcohol consumption is our liver. However, many don't understand why it causes so much damage. Our liver's job is to break down toxins and filter most of the alcohol we drink so that it can be removed from our bodies and disposed of quickly. Our liver "Runs the show" when it comes to processing alcohol; therefore, if it stops functioning due to long-term alcohol abuse, it can cause serious, life-threatening issues.

Our liver is one of the most complex organs in our body. Its functions include filtering toxins, aiding digestion, regulating blood sugar and cholesterol levels, and helping to fight infection and disease. We're heavily reliant on it, so damage caused to the liver from alcohol is often easy to spot.

Some implications of liver damage can include:

- Each time your liver filters alcohol, some of the liver cells die. The liver can develop new cells, but drinking too much over many years can reduce its regenerating ability. This can result in severe and permanent damage to our liver with the HSE

Phase 4- The healthy stuff

(Health Service Executive) claiming that 4 out of 5 deaths from liver disease are alcohol-related. Consuming lots of alcohol, even for just a few days, can lead to a build-up of fats in our liver. This is called "Alcoholic Fatty Liver Disease" and is the first stage of ARLD (alcohol-related liver disease). Fatty liver disease rarely causes any symptoms, but it's a significant warning sign that you're drinking at a harmful level. According to NHS England, an estimated 70% of people with ARLD have an alcohol dependency problem.

- Our liver metabolises alcohol, which can lead to a build-up of fat that impairs liver function. The good news? The liver is a very resilient organ and is capable of regenerating itself, so we're able to reverse a lot of the damage caused by alcohol if we choose to stop drinking for months/years at a time or decide to stop for good. The not-so-good news? Between ten to twenty percent of heavy drinkers develop a condition called cirrhosis, typically after ten or more years of drinking. Alcohol-related cirrhosis is the most severe form of ALD and occurs when the entire liver is scarred, causing the liver to shrink and harden. This could lead to liver failure, and usually, the damage cannot be reversed.

The best advice I can give to you as somebody who is by no means a doctor or health professional is to quit whilst you're ahead. I believe you already know that's

Phase 4 - The healthy stuff

the best decision for you anyway, as you're reading this book. Liver damage can begin to reverse itself in as little as 2 weeks of abstaining from alcohol - so the sooner you decide to say no, the quicker it can get started.

Heart

It's very uncomfortable to discuss the damage alcohol consumption can have on our hearts, considering it's one of, if not THE most vital organ in our body. Still, it's also essential to understand how excessive alcohol intake can damage it. This opened my eyes, so I hope it opens yours, too. This isn't to upset or make you feel distressed but to educate you. We're often naïve about the side effects drugs like alcohol have on us, as what we don't know can't hurt us, right? But there are some things we need to know before we can appreciate just how much damage it's causing and make a real change. Excessive alcohol consumption can result in various complications, some more severe than others. These include cardiomyopathy/heart failure, high blood pressure and strokes as outlined below.

- Alcohol-induced cardiomyopathy is a condition which damages your heart by causing it to change shape due to long-term heavy alcohol use. The heart stretches and enlarges, preventing it from pumping blood as well as it should and reducing our body's available oxygen supply. The changes to

Phase 4- The healthy stuff

your heart's shape causes long-term damage, leading to heart failure and severe problems. Withdrawing from alcohol may help aid recovery for some, but others will need medication or even surgery to help reverse the damage. High blood pressure is a condition closely linked to future complications such as a heart attack or stroke if it isn't controlled over time. According to the Mayo Clinic, drinking too much alcohol can raise blood pressure to unhealthy levels. Having more than three drinks in one sitting temporarily raises blood pressure. Repeated binge drinking can lead to long-term increases in blood pressure. The good news? The adverse effects from long-term drinking on your blood pressure are rapidly reversible once you stop, with blood pressure shown to begin decreasing within the first 1-3 weeks of removing alcohol, which is pretty impressive.

- Without us going into too much detail, heavy drinking can trigger a condition called "Atrial fibrillation", which is the technical term for an irregular heartbeat that can lead to blood clots forming in the heart. If one of these blood clots travels into the brain, it can cause a stroke to happen.

I appreciate how uncomfortable it might be to read through this section. I felt uncomfortable writing it. But, I cannot stress enough how many implications alcohol

Phase 4- The healthy stuff

can have on our health. I hope that this section on health has helped you to understand the impacts of drinking to excess. I am not a doctor, research scientist, or disease specialist, but I did take it upon myself to research the above.

If you wish to dive in deeper and would rather have all the facts presented to you, I recommend you do the same. Your future self will thank you for it later.

Phase 5
Financial awakening

If improving your weight, sleep, and overall health isn't enough for you to want to ditch the booze, then enhancing your finances has to do it. Drinking alcohol negatively impacts our finances significantly, but it's often something we accept and don't think to change when reassessing our spending habits, as it's seen as a necessity. Nobody seems to consider cutting out the weekly pub nights when realising their credit card bill has been considerably higher than usual. It's got to be another reason, and surely it can't be due to the round of shots I bought for a bunch of strangers last Thursday night...right? Or did the three glasses of wine I had with dinner cost more than the dinner itself? The list goes on. One thing that's always amazed me is how easy it is to spend hard-earned cash while sitting in a pub or bar,

Phase 5 - Financial awakening

and how society's whole concept of value for money quickly goes out of the window when alcohol is involved.

Money is a sensitive subject for most people, so nine times out of ten, even if somebody you know were to be in a difficult situation financially, they would do everything in their power to hide it until they really couldn't any longer. Even the people closest to us can hide it well until they need help. There is so much pride associated with money and finances. Nobody wants to tell you how much money they make, and it's always the big, fat elephant in the room.

"Nobody ever wants to tell you how much money they make, and it's always the big, fat elephant in the room."

I always thought I was useless at managing my finances and could never quite go a month without relying on a credit card or overdraft to see me through until the next payday. My young and naive self didn't quite realise then that doing this meant I was borrowing from the next month's paycheck, so the liabilities would continue to grow before my eyes. It got to a point where I knew I couldn't quite fund my lifestyle but as a young adult who had just moved to London, I honestly didn't care and thought it would all sort itself out one day.

Phase 5- Financial awakening

What I didn't plan for, however, was the slow, painful, torturous financial struggle I had to go through before getting to the point where I figured it out and had my "What the hell am I doing" moment. Don't get me wrong, I'm very grateful that I have a supportive family and know things could always be much worse; however, at a young age, I was so consumed with what was going on in my own life that I'd forget to look at the bigger picture at times. I felt so hard done by. Why do I always seem to struggle with money, but my friends don't? Why can't I make my paycheck go further? Where does all of my money go? It was clear exactly where it was going, but I ignored it. Alcohol strikes again.

> "I'm a strong believer that we all have to go on our journeys, and I'm afraid to say it, but these include the hard parts, too."

I mentioned it briefly at the start of the book; however, moving to London was like a playground, and I always seemed to find the money to go out to a party. Funnily enough, I would be okay with spending money on countless drinks and takeaways, but when it came to spending money on weekly groceries or cleaning supplies, I found it such a chore…I know, I'm shaking my head too…It just doesn't make sense. I had such tunnel vision when it came to alcohol that I saw it as a necessary cost, and it was a worthy sacrifice, but oh

Phase 5 - Financial awakening

how wrong was I? I wish I could go back and tell the Jess from 7 years ago how much of a waste all of the nights out were, but I'm a firm believer that we all have to go on our journeys, and I'm afraid to say it but these include the hard parts too. If I hadn't had the hard parts, I wouldn't have gotten to where I am now and have the clarity I have today. I wouldn't go as far as thanking the nights out, as it's fair to say they set me back quite a bit, but I needed that chapter in my life to teach me what I definitely did not want going forward, and I hope you can take comfort in this too.

> "I needed that chapter in my life to teach me what I definitely did not want going forward."

I've got way better at managing my finances now. Don't get me wrong, there will always be setbacks, but that's part of life. Certain setbacks are out of our control, and we must deal with them as they arise. The setbacks I no longer have are due to my actions and reckless spending. I no longer have to set myself back from pointless alcohol binges, frequent nights out I couldn't remember, expensive Uber rides home and excessive takeaways that often made me feel even more crap afterwards.

Now, I'd like you to picture something for me. You walk into a shop and see a turmeric and ginger shot for sale at £10. What's your immediate response to this? If I

Phase 5 - Financial awakening

were a betting man, your immediate reaction is, "No way am I spending that," and you would think it was absurd, and surely nobody in their right mind would pay this. Now, you walk up to the bar and order a cocktail; the bartender says, "That'll be £10, please, " and you don't bat an eyelid. Ironically, this option does nothing to benefit our health, and society finds it an acceptable outgoing month in and month out. Don't get me wrong, I have the utmost respect for bartenders or mixologists from a skill perspective, but paying £10+ for a cocktail in a martini glass when the cocktail is primarily orange juice and syrup is just daylight robbery, in my opinion.

"This option does nothing to benefit our health, and yet society finds it to be an acceptable outgoing month in and month out."

Alcohol can often slowly damage certain aspects of our lives over time, and our finances, I'm afraid to say, is one of them. Going out for drinks is considered the standard thing to do, so many people who are considering a life of sobriety feel that if they don't agree to go for drinks, it will impact their social lives since this is what everybody seems to want to do week in, week out. Perhaps you'd rather save money than go to the pub and spend say, £50, on drinks you don't even really want? But you feel pressured to do so to avoid feeling left out or judged. The worst part? If you're a frequent

Phase 5 - Financial awakening

drinker you'll probably find yourself spending more than this, as you don't get the same buzz as you used to from just 2-3 drinks, it now takes 4-5 to feel tipsy...

And I'm afraid to say it, but the costs never end there. We've touched on the beloved "hangover diet" in the previous chapter, however, it's not just our health and diet that suffer when the hangover diet rears its ugly head; our bank accounts also suffer. So we've spent, say £50 on the night out, £20 on the Uber/taxi home because we're too drunk to navigate public transport or leave at a reasonable time and then an additional £30 to fuel the hangover food when home and also the following day, totalling to a whopping £100 spent on one night. What happens if we repeat this just once every weekend? We're down £400 per month just like that; on nights out, we can hardly remember and have no real substance to them - mind-blowing.

> "It's not just our health and diet that suffer when the hangover diet rears its ugly head; our bank accounts suffer too."

Now, I'll be honest with you, I wish alcohol-free alternatives such as 0% beer or wine were cheaper than they are at present. I've found myself paying up to £6 for a 0% beer on some occasions, which I've never really understood, considering there is no alcohol tax on a beverage with no alcohol in it...surely? I'm still

Phase 5 - Financial awakening

trying to wrap my head around that one! At least, this is what you would think, but there we go. Even though some alcohol-free alternatives are still pretty pricey in some establishments, this isn't the case for all, and often, you'll find they are still considerably cheaper than an alcoholic beverage. Remember, it's not just the cost of the drink we're saving on but the aftermath I mentioned previously. You can drive home or take the bus, you can eat sensibly the next day or treat yourself but not in such a reckless way (as you would find yourself doing so if you were hungover), and you're unlikely to buy ten alcohol-free beers...well, you might, and it will still be cheaper than the real stuff, but I find that usually, 2-3 are enough to satisfy the stigma. And guess what? You have absolutely zero reason to start buying shots when it hits midnight! You'll likely be tucked up in bed by then with a film or a good book, as happy as Larry.

> "The times I'd turned up late to work or called in sick were some of the worst days of my life."

There is, sadly, the more severe side to the financial issues caused by alcohol consumption, which could be a loss of employment due to sick days or not turning up to work because you've slept through your alarm or are feeling too sick to show up. The financial loss from this could be significant, not to mention what this does to our mental health. Maybe you're somebody who has unfortunately experienced this before. I'm sorry if you

Phase 5 - Financial awakening

have, although I'm sure you're also aware that this is a result of your poor actions, which is why you're here. You are reading this book and are ready to turn your life around. The times I'd turned up late to work or called in sick were some of the worst days of my life. They made me feel so low, hopeless and useless. Granted, this was a very long time ago, and I'd like to think I have matured since this time. However, alcohol brings out the worst in everybody, and this can happen to anybody at any age. It truly takes no prisoners.

> "When it comes to alcohol, our concept of money is jolted."

The harsh reality is that you can very easily get fired if alcohol consumption interferes with your job performance or causes safety concerns in the workplace. Sadly, the complications don't end there. This may make it harder for you to find another job (depending on the severity of the situation), resulting in a further decline in your finances without a stable income. I would genuinely hate to see this happen to you, and I know you're better than that, so let's tackle this before you get there.

Similarly, if this has unfortunately already happened to you, I know you're here because you're ready to ensure it doesn't happen again, and you want to turn your life around and move forward, so good for you and I'm

Phase 5 - Financial awakening

happy you're here. The benefits of removing alcohol from our lives can be truly substantial when it comes to our finances in particular. Removing alcohol can allow for more savings, better financial judgement and overall better financial management and awareness, as when it comes to alcohol, our concept of money is jolted. The number of mornings I'd previously woken up from a night out and felt an overriding sense of anxiety at the thought of having to check my bank balance, knowing full well I'd spent way more than I'd planned or wanted to the evening before. Perhaps this is a feeling that sounds familiar to you, too. Sadly, it's then a slippery slope...

"Can we not make the same memories without spending a small mortgage on alcohol to fuel the night?"

One night of overspending turns into 5 nights of overspending, and our financial situation slowly declines in front of our very eyes. I appreciate that you might not be somebody who has this issue, and maybe you are in a financial situation where you can afford to fork out as much as you please for drinks at the bar without it being detrimental to you. However, I'm sharing this from my own experiences in the hope that it resonates with one or two of you readers. Please also take it with a pinch of salt as I'm sure to some degree you can resonate with the fact that you tend to spend

Phase 5 - Financial awakening

way more money when alcohol is involved than when it's not, and the money you have spent on evenings you're unable to remember likely could have been put to better use. My favourite line is, "But it's money well spent with friends and good company".

Yes, the nights you can hopefully remember lead to great memories, but can we not make the same memories without spending a small mortgage on alcohol to fuel the night? It's time to start realising that the people who love and support us are happy to spend time with us. Not a distorted, messy version of us, who often doesn't remember much of the "memorable night with friends" anyway, let's be honest.

> "Not a distorted, messy version of us, who often doesn't remember much of the "memorable night with friends.""

Since we covered it in great detail in the previous chapter, you're familiar with the severe health obstacles one can face when drinking regularly. Often, health issues need taking care of, which usually require us to purchase various medications or prescriptions which we take on a long-term basis. By eliminating alcohol, it helps us to eliminate the doctor's bills, too, since as our health improves, our need for certain medication decreases. Now, I have a little activity I

Phase 5 - Financial awakening

would like to ask you to try. Whenever you think about going to a bar or a pub within your first year of sobriety, could you put some money into a jar? Let's say the minimum is £20 because who has ever been to a bar or pub and spent less than this? Let's be honest. When you reach the end of your first year of sobriety, I want you to total up all the money within the jar and use the money to reward yourself. Rewarding yourself could mean treating yourself to a holiday, paying off some bills or putting it into your savings for a rainy day - reward looks different to us all. You'll quickly notice how much money you've saved and how much better you can use it. This exercise will also teach you the power of saying no when you have a slight moment of weakness, but in this scenario, you'll reward yourself for it later.

I would love to hear your results from completing this exercise after one year into your sobriety journey. Please don't hesitate to reach out to me if so. I cannot wait to hear your amazing stories and how you decided to use the money you've saved. Come on, let's do it for future you.

Phase 6
The hard truths

I won't pretend the journey you're about to embark on will be easy. If it were, it wouldn't be as half as rewarding. Choosing to live a life alcohol-free is challenging in the society we live in, but do you know what's tougher? Waking up every day with low self-esteem, feeling terrible within yourself 85% of the time and relying on a drug to make you feel happy for a few hours. It can be a lonely road but a truly rewarding one, and I promise you the struggle to get there will be worth it. The harsh reality is that many people who choose to live a life without alcohol try quitting on a few occasions before saying enough is enough for good. Maybe you're one of these people, and you've tried quitting a few times already; I know I certainly am. One day, it just clicked, and I decided I was too important to let a substance rule my life any longer.

Phase 6 – The hard truths

The reason it takes us a few tries before finally making a permanent change? Because it's bloody hard work. We live in a society with a solution for everything or a way to fix it. Do you need to get somewhere? You can order it and a taxi will arrive within five minutes to take you to your destination. You've run out of vitamins? Amazon Prime will have some more delivered to you the following day. You can't be bothered to cook this week? You can order all your meals pre-made at the click of a button. I'm sorry to say it, but there's no "quick fix" to curing your issues with alcohol other than removing it from your life for good, and that's the hard pill you need to swallow.

> "I'm sorry to say it, but there's no quick fix to curing your issues with alcohol and other then remove it from your life for good."

Many people try to moderate and realise that they cannot do so. Many people stop drinking and later find that they want to try and reintroduce it back into their lives, only for the same toxic cycle to rear its ugly head again in time. Our brains try to trick us into thinking, "Go on, just one drink won't hurt". Sadly, there is no such thing as "Just one drink", and if you try and convince yourself otherwise, you are potentially reopening the door into the toxic habit all over again. You and I both know you're better than that. Don't let this thought try to trick you. Perhaps you've heard that

Phase 6 - The hard truths

a "Friend of a friend" stopped drinking for a period and then was able to moderate their drinking fine afterwards. Well, I'd be shocked to find that this is the case, and the exact toxic cycle will likely creep back up on that individual again sooner or later...It's an unfortunate replay I've read about on multiple occasions. Individuals get to a point where they finally have stability without relying on alcohol, so they think, "Hmm, maybe I can give alcohol another try now, and maybe I won't be so addicted to it the next time around as I've had the break". I promise you, this is not how addiction works. If you are someone who has an issue with alcohol or has an alcohol use disorder, the sad reality is that moderating isn't an option for you as much as you may think it is or see other people moderating. I'm saying this because this is a hard truth I've sadly had to discover myself over many years of trying my best to moderate or "take it easy", and it never happening.

"By breaking the cycle, you truly get to know who you are without using alcohol as a disguise."

Amongst all of the struggles which come with having a break from alcohol or quitting altogether, you'll find it the most empowering thing you've ever done. By breaking the cycle, you genuinely get to know who you are without using alcohol as a disguise. You'll get to

Phase 6 - The hard truths

discover new hobbies you would never have even considered before when alcohol was in the picture, as all you could think about was when your next visit to the pub or bar was going to be, or what you were going to drink at the next wedding or social event. I genuinely believe we're not able to reach our full potential whilst having a relationship with alcohol because, in some way or another, it will distract you and alter your mood. Have you ever wondered how Olympians do what they do? Because they are focused and determined and know they can achieve greatness. Do you think Olympians drink alcohol? Absolutely not. Many people who have achieved greatness realised at one time or another that drinking alcohol was never going to help them get to where they needed to be, so they decided to remove it as it was a worthy sacrifice to the life they really wanted to live.

> "This chapter of your life is called taking the lost time back for you, to be the best version of you I know you can be and will be."

Now, I'm not saying you have to become an Olympian, but I'm sure you have aspired to do or achieve something that you haven't yet and likely keep putting it off or find alcohol a worthwhile distraction or excuse for not working on it. This chapter of your life is called taking the lost time back for you to be the best version of you I know you can be and will be. But to do so, you

Phase 6 - The hard truths

need to have the hard conversations, as they're the ones that genuinely matter. The first few months will be particularly tough; you probably already know that. No habit is easy to break, especially not this one, as it involves distancing yourself from all things familiar for a while, such as the places you go to, the people you know and your typical routines. But as I've said before, and I'll say multiple more times, this is the most rewarding habit you can break, as it's the one which can truly change the course of your life.

> "This is the most rewarding habit you can break."

What I find challenging might be very different from what you find difficult. However, some friends will inevitably drop away during your sobriety journey. Still, they aren't the friends you'd want to stick around anyway if they don't support you. I appreciate that this is hard to come to terms with. My close friends have stuck around, and that's all that matters.

You might find it difficult (at first) to hold conversations attending big events, which I appreciate is no fun for anybody. Alcohol gives you courage like no other, which people often rely on at big events as it can bring out an extroverted side to them they didn't even know existed, and perhaps talk to people you wouldn't even think to

Phase 6 - The hard truths

approach sober. Yes, I get that's maybe an "Advantage", but what about when you've also said something you shouldn't have to the same group of people after taking it too far? Speaking from experience, this is only something I found challenging to navigate at first, and you quickly adjust to a room full of people as a sober person. And believe it or not, it becomes far less scary and more of a superpower. Being a fun, extroverted individual is great initially, but what happens after a few hours? Things get messy and get taken a bit too far. This then quickly reverses, and the following day, the same extroverted character is left feeling anxious, embarrassed and unsettled about the very events which happened the night before.

> ## "It becomes far less scary and more of a superpower."

As for the sober version of you, this person wakes up the following day feeling rested and assured about the conversations they had the night before. They have no shame whatsoever about what had taken place, and nobody remembers the fact that they weren't even drinking. The tables quickly reverse, trust me.

When I decided to quit, I worked in a very sociable office, where there were Thursday drinks every week to ensure everybody was spending time together. I'll be

Phase 6 - The hard truths

completely honest with you, the first couple of weeks of work drinks, I dreaded attending. I would either make alternative plans or head straight home. I hadn't entirely prepared myself for the questions about why I wasn't drinking, so I decided not to deal with it at all. Yes, this isn't ideal, but this was my coping mechanism and what I needed to do to get me to the next stage of sobriety. I could sit here and say, "You need to face the challenging conversations head-on," but in reality, I don't agree with that at all. If you cast yourself back to Phase 1 of this book, you'll recall that taking a step back from familiar drinking environments is the number one rule for your first few weeks/months of sobriety. You should take as long as you need to distance yourself until you're ready to move on to the next phase.

> "All that matters is you're using a process which works well for you."

When it comes to giving up alcohol, there isn't a right or wrong way to do it - all that matters is that you're using a process which works well for you. At the time, stepping away from the Thursday office drinks was the process I needed, and when I did attend my first one a few weeks after not drinking, I felt more equipped to make it known that I was no longer drinking and would sit there with a can of coke instead. Another, let's say,

Phase 6 - The hard truths

"Challenging" part of social situations in earlier sobriety is when people try to encourage you to drink, even though you have told them that you don't want to and are happy with an alcohol-free alternative. I'd be lying to you if I said this didn't happen often, and we'll never truly understand why people feel the need to do this. I think for some people, encouraging you to "Just have one with them" makes them feel better about their insecurities when it comes to alcohol, and your deciding not to drink unintentionally makes them reflect on their relationship with drinking. It's also a way of deflecting change, as they no longer have their core drinking buddy to rely on if you aren't there making poor decisions alongside them. It's easy to enjoy an unhealthy habit when you have a friend right there with you.

"Other people's perception of you has nothing to do with how you see yourself."

You might also find the same people make remarks or digs during events. These sometimes go along the lines of "So how do you even have fun?" or "Ah, you're missing out". Whenever I've had these remarks, and speaking frankly, it thankfully hasn't happened very often, I've just ignored them as the likelihood is the person/people making the snide comments will be black-out drunk in the next hour or so anyway, so why waste the energy even entertaining it. Or please feel

Phase 6 - The hard truths

free to call them out on their *BS* if you want to and feel up to it. Sometimes, you need to have your own back and what gives these people the right to make you feel uncomfortable for making such a positive life choice? Absolutely nothing! Remember, other people's perception of you has nothing to do with how you see yourself. Your sobriety journey will teach you a whole new level of self-love, where you begin to pity the people who make digs or remarks rather than worry about how they perceive you. Trust me - you've got this. Another hard truth to deal with about sobriety is that you might find yourself feeling bored at first, which is normal.

> "If you also try something that doesn't quite work out and you're not enjoying it, there are hundreds of others you can try until one sticks."

We've touched on just how many wasted nights you've spent at the pub, to spend the following day then hungover, well you're about to get all of that time back (for future you anyway) but have no real idea as to what you should be doing with it, at first. Suddenly, you have all of this free time, yet your friends still do their usual routines of wasting the day at the pub. Well, my best advice is to get stuck into something new as quickly as possible, to alleviate lonely feelings and to start

Phase 6 - The hard truths

getting to know the new, amazing, unique version of yourself. A sports club is a great way to do this, as sport is something everybody can benefit from and there are so many different activities available for you to enjoy. If you also try something that doesn't quite work out and you're not enjoying it, there are hundreds of others you can try until one sticks.

A topic we haven't touched upon yet, but I feel it's very vital that we do, is what happens when you first remove alcohol from your diet. Don't get me wrong, the rewards and benefits do come much quicker than expected; however, I wouldn't be doing my job without presenting all the facts to you and making you aware of the potential withdrawal period you may have to deal with, sometimes lasting up to 1 week.

> "The more you drink regularly, the more you're likely to be affected by withdrawal symptoms."

Speaking from experience, I don't recall having any noticeable withdrawal symptoms when I decided to stop drinking. However, I'm very aware that this period looks different for everybody and varies heavily on how much alcohol you consume. I would classify myself as a frequent social drinker who drank 2-3 times per week - the more you drink regularly, the more you're likely to be affected by withdrawal symptoms. These symptoms are part of a condition called 'Alcohol Withdrawal

Phase 6 - The hard truths

Syndrome', which is a reaction caused when our bodies become dependent on alcohol but are then deprived of it and try to adjust. Symptoms can be physical and psychological and range from mild to severe.

Typical symptoms of alcohol withdrawal may include:

- Hand tremors ('the shakes')
- Sweating
- A raised pulse rate (above 100 beats per minute)
- Nausea/Vomiting
- Headaches
- Loss of appetite
- Depression/Anxiety Irritability

Now, if you're thinking what I'm thinking, then the majority of these symptoms I'd undoubtedly get during a weekly hangover - if not all of them. What is the difference in this scenario? This is hopefully the last time you'll ever have to deal with them if you choose to opt for a permanent state of sobriety.

If you do happen to experience withdrawal symptoms, here are some tips which may help relieve them:

- Try to avoid drinking too much caffeine and keep yourself hydrated with plenty of non-alcoholic drinks (just in case that wasn't clear...)

Phase 6 – The hard truths

- Try to eat regularly and have a healthy, balanced diet (plenty of carbs, vegetables and protein).

- Find ways to relax, like reading, walking, listening to music, mindfulness, exercise or meditation.

- Seek support and company from non-dependent friends and family. An outside perspective can be beneficial and provide comfort.

I genuinely hope you don't experience any withdrawal symptoms, but if you do, please know that this is only temporary and the bigger picture is so much brighter, and this is all part of the process. If you're struggling within the first weeks, take it back to basics and remember the main goal is to handle your symptoms in productive ways that work for you. Plan to learn new coping strategies and create new daily routines. Please remember, when taking on any journey, the first steps are often the hardest, and the only way is up afterwards – you've got this.

My last hard truth? And this one is big, so brace yourself. A voice inside will keep telling you, "It's too hard", and maybe you should "Revert to your old ways", but you must ignore and fight it as this is nonsense. Your brain may also trick you into thinking you're bored, and introducing alcohol back into your life will add a bit of excitement, which couldn't be further from the truth.

Phase 6 - The hard truths

It will only fuel more of the self-destructive behaviour you have been working so hard to throw away.

We're often told our brains know what's best for us, but contrary to popular opinion, this couldn't be further from the truth. Daily habits engrained over time program our brains, so when we decide to quit drinking, it will set off some alarm bells. It's out of character and the ordinary course of business. Not only is it out of character, but the brain also likes alcohol as it releases more dopamine (the chemical linked with pleasure and satisfaction). Not to mention, it's a drug and heavily addictive, as you already know.

> "The first steps are often the hardest when taking any journey."

We must retrain our brains to focus on a new routine and break the old one. You'll often hear people say that the first 90 days of sobriety are the most important, purely because this is where the most vital changes and determination have to take place. Once you pass the 90 days, things get a lot easier. My advice? Focus on one day at a time, and remember to reward yourself. Make sure you remind yourself at the end of every day, "I'm proud of myself. I stayed sober today", and before you know it, 1 day will turn into 30 days, then 90 days, and you'll suddenly forget to keep count as you're happy in

Phase 6 – The hard truths

your new routine with no booze in sight.

Change is always challenging. If it weren't, everybody would do it. But that's what sets you apart from others. You have the fight in you to fight for the life you want and know you deserve. A life aside from alcohol, which has turned you into a version of yourself that is the total opposite of the person you want to be, time and time again.

I know you're a boss, which is why I'm preparing you for the hard parts of sobriety. I want you to conquer this, as I know you deserve it.

Phase 7
Reaping the rewards

If I haven't made it evident by now that the rewards of living a life of sobriety are truly endless, then I'm certainly about to.

When we say reaping the rewards, what do we mean? If you look up the definition of reward, it is defined as "The thing given in recognition of service, effort or achievement", and you choosing to live a life of sobriety is all the above. It's recognition of the service you have put into yourself and your growth. It's the endless effort of telling yourself you don't need a substance which has proven to be so destructive to your well-being time and time again, even on the days when it feels much harder

Phase 7 - Reaping the rewards

to say no. It's recognising how far you've come and achieved in your sobriety journey. It's called a journey for a reason, as this is no easy thing to crack, but it indeed can be the most rewarding thing you'll ever do. Amongst all the obstacles, all the outside noise, the inner voice inside of you trying to trick you into thinking you're not worthy of anything more, you stuck to your word and didn't turn back, and the power this holds is like no other.

> *"It's called a journey for a reason, as this is no easy thing to crack, but it truly can be the most rewarding thing you'll ever do."*

The reality is that the rewards will happen naturally once you opt for a life of sobriety, and that's the most rewarding part of it all - things start to improve automatically once you begin to say no and choose yourself. According to a survey carried out by the University of Sussex, where 1,000 people tried giving up alcohol for a month, it was found that:

- 93% felt a sense of achievement
- 88% saved money
- 70% had generally improved health
- 70% slept better
- 67% had more energy
- 58% lost weight
- 57% had better concentration
- 54% had better skin

Phase 7 - Reaping the rewards

I don't know about you, but I find these results to be pretty exceptional - especially from just one month of sobriety...one! So, the rewards genuinely do speak for themselves. We've covered some hard truths, and we've also covered the health and financial benefits, which, don't get me wrong, are no short of fantastic, but do you know what else is? Feeling like you again and getting to rediscover new parts of yourself aside from alcohol and regaining your power.

> "You'll suddenly start to feel invincible as you regain your passion for life again."

The most rewarding part of this journey is its benefits on your mind and soul. The benefits only you can experience as they happen deep within. When you choose to say no to alcohol and start saying yes to yourself, you begin to build trust in yourself again and no longer seek external validation. If you can conquer this, I genuinely believe there's not much you won't be able to conquer, and you'll suddenly start to feel invincible as you regain your passion for life. What is more rewarding than proving to yourself just how strong you are and that you're not going to let anything get in the way of you consistently showing up for yourself day in and day out to ensure you're the best version of yourself, for yourself. Not only will you see all the amazing benefits we've discussed come to light, but others will notice the positive changes within you

Phase 7 - Reaping the rewards

too, and will start treating you with a different level of respect. When you start showing up for yourself, others must change how they show up for you, too. It might be that you're no longer a pushover or people-pleaser, or don't let things slide that the previous version of you would've quickly done so.

> "You'll have greater mental clarity, and what you want for yourself and your life will soon become clearer."

People may not respond to this well, but the ones who do are the ones you know are the people you want in your life and want to stick around. Not only will others start treating you better, but you'll also have greater mental clarity, and what you want for yourself and your life will soon become more apparent. You no longer have alcohol there as a distraction and have done the self-work to get to a place where you're ready to think about what you want out of life and which direction you'd like to pursue going forward. Whereas before, I'm sure many of you feel that all you could think about was making it through the day without feeling negatively about yourself, as I know that can be challenging.

There are so many ways our mental health improves when we quit drinking. Many of these happen naturally as our judgement is no longer clouded, allowing us to focus more on the positive rather than the doom and gloom.

You might find some of the benefits include:

- **Increased clarity:** Sobriety allows us to think more clearly and make better decisions, leading to a healthier self-image and awareness. Our mental health begins to improve as we no longer participate in the events which cause us to feel triggered and riddled with regret due to the consequences of poor choices.

- **Freedom from regret:** It's no secret that the majority of us have done things we regret whilst under the influence of alcohol, leaving us with feelings of guilt and shame for a period, which never really leaves us entirely until we stop drinking. When your mind is no longer filled with this kind of remorse, it frees up space for you to fill your thoughts with more positive, self-affirming thoughts.

- **Emotional Stability:** As mentioned previously, alcohol is a depressant; therefore, it's only natural that it heightens negative emotions, causing us to spiral, act irrationally and have negative mood swings often. Quitting alcohol allows us to experience more emotional stability, allowing room

Phase 7 - Reaping the rewards

for our thoughts and feelings to rebalance themselves without a negative influence clouding our judgment.

- **Increased self-reflection:** Quitting alcohol allows us the time and space to do the inner work, as mentioned in the previous chapters. Without having it there as a constant distraction, it means we can focus on building a stronger sense of self-worth and appreciation for ourselves, unravelling the anxiety, insecurity and lack of self-esteem alcohol use has likely caused us over the years.

I would love to sit here and promise you that you will see all of the benefits and rewards come to life within the first week of choosing a life of sobriety, but this isn't realistic. I'm here to present you with the facts, not blindside you with unrealistic expectations. All I ask of you is that you be patient with yourself and take it day by day.

> "You'll soon snap back into boss mode after realising you had a slight moment of weakness."

On the days you're struggling a little more than others and go to reach for that drink, please say to yourself, "No, I can do this for just one more day" as I promise you, that's a decision you will never regret. You'll soon

Phase 7 - Reaping the rewards

snap back into boss mode after realising you had a slight moment of weakness. If this does happen, please do not worry. We are only human, and knowing that you could have caved at that moment will make you stronger. You chose to be sober for one more day.

There are certainly proven benefits from as little as 1 week after calling it quits with alcohol, the big one being to sleep and how you feel so much more rested. However, it's important to note that everybody is different, and the results can differ from person to person. Some people experience beneficial changes to their minds and bodies more rapidly than others, but this doesn't mean they aren't on their way to you, too.

There are various factors to consider when we discuss the timeline of receiving the benefits and rewards of withdrawing from alcohol, and multiple factors influence the timescales for each individual.

> "The first few months aren't without its challenges but also come with noticeable rewards."

For example, if you quit drinking but eat junk food 3 times a day, the likelihood is your weight isn't going to change as much as somebody who is, say, treating themselves to a takeaway once a week. What I do know for sure, is if you stick to your usual diet (minus the

Phase 7 – Reaping the rewards

hangover binges) but remove alcohol from it, you will see a noticeable difference in your weight in a short space of time. If you stay up late binging Netflix until 2 a.m., your sleep won't improve as much as somebody who goes to sleep at a reasonable time, and of course, you won't feel as rested. I'm sure you get the gist. The first few months aren't without challenges but also come with noticeable rewards.

Typically, according to research, the timeline is likely to go as follows:

Week 1-2

Symptoms of withdrawal are possible, if not likely (as we touched on in phase 6), as you adjust to the absence of alcohol. This is subject to the amount of alcohol you consume and will vary from person to person. Your overall mental clarity improves from week 2 as your sleep improves and you feel more relaxed and rested. Many people describe this period as the "fog lifting" as your mornings suddenly become easier and enjoyable, your mood balances, and you start to look and feel refreshed.

Week 3-4

Your energy levels will start to improve, and you'll likely notice changes to your weight and physical

Phase 7 - Reaping the rewards

appearance as you now have more energy to focus on exercising regularly and eating nourishing foods. Your financials will start improving, too. Since you've saved 3-4 weeks of not wasting money at the pub or the supermarket on pointless drinks - go you! You're starting to really enjoy your new routine and notice significant improvements to your overall mental health, including reduced stress, anxiety, and depression. You'll likely feel a sense of control over your health and a sense of accomplishment from staying sober for a whole month. You've proved to yourself that you have what it takes and are now enjoying snippets of the rewards. You're proud of how far you've come, and it's just the beginning.

⌄

Weeks 5-6

Improvements to your physical health and well-being are highly noticeable, and you look and feel better in yourself, and others can notice it, too. Your internal organs are repairing themselves and beginning to recover as you leave the detox stage of early sobriety. You suddenly have a new perspective and outlook on life and start to reflect on your past behaviours and relationships. Yes, it might feel slightly lonely at times, and you still might be battling with certain urges to "Go for one", but you know you're smarter than to be tricked

Phase 7 - Reaping the rewards

into old ways. You're excited and optimistic about discovering the new you now that you've tasted how good sobriety looks on you.

Weeks 7-8

You've developed a healthy strategy for dealing with triggers and stress, and you feel comfortable on your path and the direction your life is going in. You might be ready to revisit familiar drinking places, but you're visiting as the new you with a new perspective on life and don't need a toxic habit to invade your space any longer. You've started a new hobby which you're enjoying and have begun connecting with new people. You're consistent with your routine and continue to show up for yourself as you continue the journey of self-discovery.

Weeks 9-12

This is a time of deep reflection as you approach the three-month window of sobriety. You're proud of yourself for how far you've come in such a short period and for dealing with the challenges. Everything in your life is improving from your physical and mental health,

Phase 7 - Reaping the rewards

appearance, your health and well-being, finances, and relationships, and you're excited about your future. You know the journey is far from over, but you know the most challenging part is, and now it's time to start enjoying life truly and what you can make of it. You're planning and developing key skills to prolong your sobriety, hopefully well into the future. This is the time to enjoy the new you and build on the foundation you've worked hard to rebuild over the past few months.

≫

Months 3-6

You've built a foundation and solidified a commitment to a sober lifestyle, laying the groundwork for continued benefits. You feel resilient, strong, proud and have developed a real trust in yourself and feel you can tackle whatever you set your mind to as you've tackled one of the hardest things of them all - choosing to stay sober in a society which is based solely around alcohol. You're beginning to inspire others as they see the benefits that not drinking is having on you and want some of the pie, too. You feel empowered and enlightened and have faith in yourself that the journey is going to continue to get better from here as you continue to work on yourself and your future.

Phase 7 - Reaping the rewards

Once you've gotten through the first 3-6 months of sobriety, I genuinely think you'll start seeing the rewards of sobriety come to life in every way, and you'll realise there's no going back as the old version of you no longer serves you anymore. You've had a real taste of what sobriety can offer you, so why would you want to look back? Everything is improving right before your very eyes and it will only continue to improve as you do the inner work and keep showing up for yourself.

Whenever there are times that you have a moment of weakness, all it takes is to go back to basics and deal with the moment in front of you and what is in your control rather than focusing too much on the future. Focus your attention onto what you can control within that very moment, then within the next hour, and then the next day, and suddenly you'll feel recentred again.

Phase 8
Never look back

Now we've reached the final section of the book, I want you to reflect on what we've covered for just a moment. From self-development, physical health, mental health, the people we surround ourselves with and our finances. What do all these things have in common? They are the foundations that decide the kind of life we choose to live, the type of person we choose to be, and the legacy we choose to leave behind. We've covered all the eye-opening facts about alcohol and that it can damage every single area of our lives if we choose to let it.

Choosing to say no to alcohol means you are choosing to say yes to yourself and your future because you want to live a life you are the boss of, and only you get to

Phase 8 - Never look back

decide how it turns out. I mentioned at the start of the book that choosing to go alcohol-free may be something you only wish to do for a short period, so when I say never look back, I fully appreciate a life of sobriety long term might not be your intention. Perhaps you still don't wish to rule it out completely, even after reading this book. But when I say never look back, this goes for you too. Even if you intend on only having a short break, what this brief break from alcohol will give you is the power to learn self-control, the power to say no and a period to reset and reflect. This in turn will break the toxic cycle with alcohol I believe you are in if you've gotten this far.

> *"Even if you intend on only having a short break, what this short break from alcohol will give you is the power to learn self-control."*

As an advocate for sobriety, I can only hope that the benefits of going alcohol-free will be so positive and impactful that it encourages you to stay sober for longer than you initially had planned. That being said, it's a decision only you can make. Research suggests that those who complete 30 days of sobriety are more likely to extend the sobriety period due to the results speaking for themselves and not wanting to revert to old ways. To truly understand what sobriety can do for you, you need to hear it straight from the horse's mouth, so here it goes. The past year of my life has been the most eye-opening year I've ever had. It's been a year of great self-reflection, self-development and growth. Yes, it's been the most challenging year of my life in so many ways, but it's also been one of the best years of my life. I feel such a whirlwind of emotions whilst I write this, and I can honestly say I'm so proud of myself for deciding to quit alcohol and trusting myself enough to stick to it.

> "It's been the most challenging year of my life in so many ways, but it's also been one of the best years of my life."

If I sit and reflect for just a second and picture what my life would be like at this very moment if I hadn't chosen to give sobriety a real shot. I see a woman who is still highly insecure, not happy within herself or her body, has self-destructive thoughts regularly, acts recklessly and has an overarching fear that she's wasting her life away. She worries that this is all there is to life and that she doesn't deserve anything more because alcohol will do that to you. She's afraid she's not where she's supposed to be and is a failure. All because she doesn't have the job of her dreams, she doesn't have kids or isn't married and she spends all her free time at the pub or bar with people who have no idea of the challenges she faces within. And the worst part? She'd probably be thinking every day how the world would be a much

Phase 8 - Never look back

better place if she wasn't in it, and that's a tough pill to swallow. She worries that she might not even be here if she let certain dark thoughts get the better of her. But what if I reflect on myself as she is today, after twelve months alcohol-free? She feels powerful, self-assured and confident. She knows she doesn't have all the answers, but she's trying her best. Yes, she's made many mistakes, but she no longer cares because mistakes are part of life and will only make her stronger in the long run. She doesn't know what the future holds, but she knows that whatever happens, she has her own back, loves herself for who she is now and doesn't focus on the version in the past.

> *"She feels powerful, self-assured and confident. She knows she doesn't have all the answers, but she's trying her best."*

Yes, looking back can be helpful, but there's nothing there for her anymore, and our new strategy is to focus on the present whilst building a dream future that she and those she chooses to be a part of it can be proud of. The sobriety journey continues and will likely always continue, as an issue with alcohol is part of who she is, but it doesn't define her. It's part of the jigsaw puzzle of her life that needed to slot in so she could continue building the bigger, beautiful masterpiece. These two versions of me couldn't be further away from each other and I honestly believe this is due to removing one key

Phase 8 - Never look back

catalyst, alcohol. It has changed my entire perspective on life, and I no longer see the glass as half empty. If I'm able to make this progress in just twelve months of sobriety, think what you can do, too. Alcohol clouds our judgement and tricks us into thinking it's helping us cope with everyday struggles, but in reality, it does everything but.

I want you to think of yourself today and what parts of this version of you you'd like to change if you could. This isn't to speak negatively to ourselves; it's the first part of understanding what we don't like about ourselves to understand our starting point for change.

> "You've gotten this far and should be extremely proud of that - it's a huge step forward."

Now that you've thought about those pieces, I'd like you to write them down on the notes pages which follow on from this chapter and bid them farewell, as this is the day you leave the present behind and embark on your next chapter. It's okay if you don't feel ready to take this step. The pages will still be here to use when you are ready. You've gotten this far and should be incredibly proud - it's a huge step forward.

Today is the day I hope you choose yourself and start your sobriety journey. I hope you never look back, but

Phase 8 - Never look back

if you do, I hope you read what you've written on the notes pages of this book and find you barely recognise that person anymore.

Please do not only me but yourself a favour and become the sobriety boss I absolutely know you can and will become, for it will be the best choice you will ever make.

NOTES

Today, I'm choosing to leave behind...

_____

_____

_____

_____

_____

_____

_____

_____

Thank you for reading!

If you enjoyed reading this self help book, please kindly leave a review on www.amazon.com

About the Author

Jessica is 29 and originally from Bristol, in the South West of England. She has lived in London for over 8 years and has worked in various fields, before very recently turning to writing and self-development after discovering her newfound sobriety.

"How to quit alcohol like a boss and live a life of sobriety" is Jessica's first book, but she intends to build a library around sobriety, self-development, and societal pressures amongst many other topics.

Jessica wants to support and encourage people to become the best versions of themselves and hopes that her books will provide a good starting point for individuals to go on to do just that.